MOZART

MOZART

(*From the portrait by Lange*)

MOZART

BY

SACHEVERELL SITWELL

WITH A FRONTISPIECE

 BOOKS FOR LIBRARIES PRESS
FREEPORT, NEW YORK

First Published 1932
Reprinted 1970

STANDARD BOOK NUMBER:
8369-5300-2

LIBRARY OF CONGRESS CATALOG CARD NUMBER:
71-114896

PRINTED IN THE UNITED STATES OF AMERICA

CONTENTS

5

IN
MEMORY OF
MRS. SAMUEL COURTAULD
FOR HER LOVE OF
MUSIC

I

CHILDHOOD—1756-1771

A BOOK upon Mozart, if it is to meet with any degree of success, must appeal to several sorts of readers. Even those unlucky few who cordially dislike music cannot help being interested in him, merely as a phenomenon. That makes one class of person, and then there is another who dismisses him as being altogether too eighteenth century, an affair of airs and graces, of tinkling melody and facile ornament. These are the people who say they prefer Bach, but when they turn away from the greatest artist of the Rococo age do they realize they are venturing into the most formal and diffuse architecture of the Baroque period? They will deny this, but it is true ; and yet how easily Mozart will win them back again with his clear and simple beauties !

And, finally, there are those to whom everything that Mozart wrote is sacred and wonderful. They were won over, long ago, by some

ravishment of the ears in a church, or they
heard that incredible grace and delicacy in
some concert-hall, or even on a gramophone.
It could be nothing but Mozart, unless it were
Haydn, and Haydn leads quickly and of his
own will, obviously, into Mozart. After this,
they will go anywhere to hear his music, but
there is such a lot of it that they cannot be expected to find their way about. Perhaps it is
true that no one can hope to hear more than half
of Mozart. Now this eager, if a little helpless,
sort of audience is the general public, and this
book is primarily meant for these. That it is
written by a complete and uninitiated amateur
must be his apology to one half of the audience
and his qualification to the other part of it.

With Mozart, more than with any other
artist, one must begin at the beginning, and
so, having stated that this first chapter must,
of necessity, consist almost entirely of anecdotes
of his childhood and its prodigies, we can start,
straight away, with the date of his birth. He
was born at Salzburg, on 27th January 1756,
and was given the names of Johannes Chryso-
stomus Wolfgang Theophilus, but in later life
he liked to be known as Wolfgang Amade.
His father, Leopold Mozart, was violin-master
to the Prince-Archbishop of Salzburg. Leopold

was dutiful, conscientious, respectable, and dull ; nevertheless he had published in the year of Wolfgang's birth a treatise on the violin which formed the basis of violin-playing in Germany during the whole of the latter part of the eighteenth century. His numerous musical compositions were of no merit whatever. His importance was his son, and he quickly realized it.

The mother was Anna Maria Pertl, or Bertlin, daughter of another official of the Archbishop's Court. Wolfgang's birth nearly cost his mother her life. It is clear that he inherited his gaiety from her, for there was little of it in his father. They had seven children, but only two of them survived, Wolfgang and his sister Maria Anna, ' Nannerl.' He was devoted to his parents and adored his sister, who was his elder by five years. She, also, had astonishing musical facility, and when he was three years old Wolfgang began to take an interest in his sister's music-lessons. That started him, and from the age of three he never stopped.

Nannerl was learning the clavier, and Wolfgang used to perch himself at her side and amuse himself by finding out thirds which he would strike with every sign of delight. He would remember the more prominent passages

9

in the pieces that he heard, and he learned to compose at the same time that he learned to play. Soon he could perform little pieces with perfect correctness and in exact time. A music-book in the Mozarteum at Salzburg has minuets and an air with twelve variations with a note in Leopold's handwriting to the effect that Wolf-gangerl learned these pieces in his fourth year. Later on, in this same music-book, come the words, ' This minuet and trio were learned by Wolfgangerl in half an hour, at half-past nine at night, on 26th January 1761, one day before his fifth year.'

His father had begun teaching him in fun, but was now serious about it. Wolfgang thought of nothing else and was only happy at the clavier. The only other thing he liked was mathematics, a science that we are told is closely akin—though how different !—to music. This, also, would absorb him, for we read that when he was learning arithmetic, tables, stools, walls, and even the floor were chalked over with figures.

The time had now come to show his two prodigies to advantage, and the father started to take Nannerl and Wolfgang on a little tour with him. In the summer of 1762 they went to Munich, and later on in the same year to

Vienna. Their travels had begun, and this was the beginning of Wolfgang's fame.

On their way to Vienna, at the monastery of Ips, while their travelling companions, two Minorite friars and a Benedictine, were saying mass, Wolfgang stole up to the organ-loft and played so admirably that the Franciscan friars of the monastery and some guests they were entertaining in the refectory rose from table and ran in, open-mouthed, to listen to him. Outside Vienna there was some trouble with the douane, but Wolfgang played them a minuet on his little violin, showed them his harpsichord, and got the family safely through the Customs without more ado.

No wonder his father loved him ; but so did everyone else who met him. He had the simplest, prettiest ways imaginable, craved for affection, and would ask his father and mother, or Nannerl, a dozen times a day if they loved him.

He was taken to Court. The Hapsburgs had a traditional and inherited love of music to which the Empress Maria Theresa, the last of her line, was no exception. When they were received, Nannerl wore a white silk Court-dress and Wolfgang a violet-coloured suit trimmed with broad gold braid. After he had played he would spring on the Empress's lap, throw his arms round her neck and kiss her, and play with the little Archduchesses on a footing of perfect equality. He especially liked Marie Antoinette. She picked him up once, when he tumbled on the polished floor, and he called out to her, ' You are good. I will marry you.' He was asked ' Why ? ' by the Empress, and he replied, ' She was kind to me. Her sister stood by and did nothing.'

Of course if the Empress received little Wolfgang all other doors were open to him. The Countess Leopold Kinsky even put off on his account a party she was to have given for Field-Marshal Daun, a great soldier of the day who had been Viceroy of Naples and who had a different coat for every day of the year.

Soon after this the Mozart family went back to Salzburg, but they started off again, before long, on a much more extended scheme of travels. They were going to the German Courts, to Paris, and even to London. On their way through Germany they heard the Mannheim orchestra, the best of its day, which must have been a revelation to Wolfgang, and they gave concerts at Frankfurt. At one of these the young Goethe was among the audience. ' I saw him as a boy seven years old,' he told Eckermann. ' I, myself, was fourteen, and I remember the little fellow distinctly with his powdered wig and his sword.'

At Brussels, on the 14th of October 1763, Wolfgang wrote his first sonata. He was seven and a half years old, and a few weeks later, when they got to Paris, it was engraved and published with three more sonatas arranged with accompaniment for violin. Meanwhile, the Mozart family had become the fashion and the print-shops were flooded with their portraits. On New Year's Eve they were received at Versailles during the Royal banquet. They, alone, had the way cleared before them, and they marched through the crowd, behind the Swiss Guard, to the side of Louis xv. and his Queen. But little Wolfgang did not take to the Pompadour. He was standing on a table and she turned her head away, and refused to kiss him. ' Who is this who won't kiss me ? ' he cried. ' My Empress kissed me.' Perhaps he had overheard his father's opinion of the French. This is how Leopold wrote of them. ' The ladies wear their clothes trimmed with fur in summer as well as winter ; they wear fur round their necks, fur round their arms, and fur in their hair instead of flowers. Pomp and splendour are extravagantly pursued and

13

admired by the men. Their money is chiefly spent on Lucretias, who, however, do not stab themselves.'

Next after Paris came London, and they reached it in April 1764, and took rooms in Frith Street, Soho. They had never seen the sea before. Nannerl noted in her diary, ' How the sea-water runs away and comes back again.' A fortnight later they were playing before the King and Queen and were rewarded with a present of twenty-four guineas.

The next week Their Majesties bowed to them in St. James's Park from their carriage. The Mozart family were on foot, but King George threw down the window, put out his head, and greeted them, laughingly, with head and hands. The Mozart family stayed, altogether, over a year in England. They appeared on numerous occasions at Vauxhall and Ranelagh, at public concerts, and at parties in private houses. A musical amateur, the Hon. Daines Barrington, gives a delightful account of Wolfgang at one of these. ' Whilst playing to me,' he writes, ' a favourite cat came in, on which he left his harpsichord, nor could we bring him back for a considerable time. He would, also, run about the room with a stick between his legs by way of horse.'

All through these months he was busily composing little pieces for the clavier, sonatas, and even small symphonies. He had made friends with John Christian Bach, son of the great John Sebastian, and music-master to the Queen, and it was his first contact with the ornate Italian style of music. He must have been influenced by this friendship, but his progress was now interrupted for a time by the illness of all his family. Leopold caught a quinsy and nearly died of it, while, a short time after his recovery, when the family had removed to Holland, Nannerl had such an alarming illness that her life was despaired of, and Wolfgang fell ill with a serious inflammatory fever.

This was the worst of their continual travels, but the first big tour was nearly over, and by the end of 1766 they were back home in Salzburg. Not for long, though ; they were off again, much too soon, to Vienna, and, as a result of that, both Nannerl and Wolfgang caught the smallpox. On his last visit to Vienna he had been ill with scarlet fever. The wonder is that his eyesight was not fatally impaired. For all his father's affection, Wolfgang was bundled about from town to town, like an exhibit at a fair. Speaking of one of these journeys, Leopold writes that he does not wish to postpone it until Wolfgangerl has reached the age and stature which will deprive his accomplishments of all that is marvellous. In fact, his father expected little enough of him when his precocity was no longer an object of wonder.

This gives a double pathos to the thought of all the fatigues undergone by the poor child. Indeed, his health in later life was seriously affected by these early hardships, for it may be said that Mozart had hardly a moment's rest from the time he was four years old until the day he died. His stamina was never given a chance of strengthening itself. Before he had fully recovered from the smallpox he was back in Vienna writing his first opera, La Finta Semplice. A little comic opera, Bastien et Bastienne, followed closely on this. He was scarcely twelve years old. Soon afterwards he had begun writing his first masses, and all the time he was pouring out a continual stream of serenades, cassations, divertimenti, sonatas for piano and violin, and pieces for the clavier.

The next thing was Italy, for Leopold thought that his son was old enough, and sufficiently sure of himself, to risk an encounter with the greatest musicians of the world. Besides, he would learn from them. With these ends in view they set out for Italy, in December 1769, and made for Bologna. The attraction was Padre Martini, the greatest contrapuntist and musical-theorist of the day. The old gentleman took the deepest and kindest interest in Wolfgang, and later on, when he came back to Bologna, after a most severe and trying examination Wolfgang was elected member of the Philharmonic Society, a very great honour. He met Farinelli, the foremost castrato singer of all time, who was living in retirement outside Bologna ; and, meanwhile, at Florence, he had made friends with an English boy, Thomas Lindley, a sort of Chatterton of music, and an undoubted genius, who was most unfortunately drowned in England when only twenty years old.

The Mozarts went to Rome also, and to Naples. At Rome, Wolfgang accomplished his celebrated feat of copying down from memory Allegri's Miserere, a complicated polyphonic piece only performed by the Papal choir during Holy Week, and the secrecy of which was kept inviolate by the threat of excommunication.

They travelled to Naples in company with four Augustinian monks, and, on arrival, visited the English Ambassador, and heard the famous

Lady Hamilton perform on the clavier with 'unusual expression.' Leopold wore a coat of maroon-coloured watered silk with sky-blue velvet facings, and Wolfgang an apple-green coat with rose-coloured facings and silver buttons. His letters home are full of sharp observation and study of character. He writes: 'The opera here is by Jomelli, it is beautiful, but the dances are miserably pompous. The King (Ferdinando IV.) has the coarse Neapolitan manner, and when he is at the opera always stands on a stool in order to look a little taller than the Queen. Vesuvius is smoking furiously to-day.'

Honours crowded in upon Wolfgang. He was made member of the Philharmonic Academy of Verona, and was knighted by the Pope with the cross of the Order of the Golden Spur. But, in spite of all this, his Italian journeys were not quite all the success they might have been, for Wolfgang's operas, or, at least, operatic works, though highly praised, did not lead to any really important engagements. There had been three of them, Mitridate, Ascanio in Alba, and Lucio Scilla, but the failure of the last-named, which was produced in Milan, in December 1772, a whole year after he had returned to Salzburg, marks the close of the first

18

period of his life, of his childhood, in fact, for, a month after this, he was seventeen years old.

Had it succeeded, he would have become acclimatized as an Italian composer, as did many German musicians of the time, Hasse, for instance. His whole career ran into other channels, but it is impossible to overestimate the effect upon him of all the Italian music that he had heard. It is a world of dead beauty to us in our century. What do we know of their church-music, or of the old opera seria, or the opera buffa, of Naples? The elder Scarlatti, Leonardo Leo, Jomelli, they are only names to us, but they formed an integral part of Mozart's experience, and with Mozart, as with Bach, it is impossible to emphasize too much the amount to which he was influenced by men whose work has been neglected and forgotten by us. We must take it for granted, that is all, that Mozart came back to Salzburg fortified with all the wiles, the tricks of perspective, and the natural poetry of the Italian genius. Italian music, and music only, he had centred his mind upon during all those months away from home, for it is true that there is no mention in any of his letters of the pictures or buildings admired by all average travellers. He was no 'virtuoso,' in that old sense of the word ; but he came back from Italy heavy-laden and ripe with experience. His childhood was over and his youth had begun.

II

THE ROCOCO PERIOD—1771-1781

THE next period of his life we have called the
Rococo age. It was from now that the earliest
of his compositions entered into the repertory.
We have to take for granted all that he had
accomplished so far, for there is so seldom an
opportunity of hearing it. In some ways it
was the most difficult part of his life. He was
no longer a child prodigy. He must astonish
the public with other things than his youth.
Would he emerge and become a great artist?
An incredible fertility, an unheard-of delicacy
of finish, these are the qualities that we see
altering, gradually, into the inspired miracles
written by him in his early twenties. For there
were moments, even with Mozart, when everything was in doubt. We are reminded of what
a friend had written to Dr. Burney years before
from Salzburg, who said, ' If I may judge of
the music which I heard of his composition,
in the orchestra, he is one further instance of

early fruit being more extraordinary than excellent.'

About this time, 1773 and 1774, he was for some fifteen months in Salzburg, and this is a good opportunity to say a little about the world, that German world of the eighteenth century, in which Mozart was living. It was split into two, Protestant and Catholic; and if Bach is the epitome of one half of it, Mozart gives the character of the other. But this is too simple a statement, for Bach was the only supreme artist produced by the Protestant world, in the strict keeping of its principles, while Mozart was not, really, so isolated a figure as we might suppose. Bach, the greatest in so many ways of all the artists of Europe, lived, unconscious of his tremendous eminence, in exactly the world we may imagine for him. Streets of wooden houses, gabled and brightly painted, flocks of geese, provincial importances in exaggerated bag-wigs; not a single painter, or poet, or architect within miles; in fact, the mediaeval Germany, untouched and unaltered. Frederick the Great was to change this, but he had hardly arrived by 1750, the year of Bach's death.

Mozart, on the other hand, lived midway between French and Italian influences. French architects and craftsmen worked in

Bavaria ; Italians worked everywhere, Bavaria and Austria as well. We have said that Mozart was not interested in these other arts, but he was the child of his age and these things were very much in the air. It was a minor age, but an age of excellence none the less, as anyone will agree who has seen the great monasteries of St. Florian and Melk on the Austrian Danube, or Ottobeuren and Weltenburg in Southern Germany. The good architects of the time, Prandauer, J. M. Fischer, the Dientzenhofers, the Asam brothers, grew along with Mozart, and they help to explain him. He was no more isolated among the visual than the oral arts.

Also, it must be kept in mind that Mozart, before he was eight years old, had played to the Courts of Vienna, Paris, and London, and, however stupid Royal persons may have been, they were, at least, still surrounded by trappings of a fabulous elegance and grace. If we add to these impressions of his earliest childhood all the experience of his Italian tours, in the greatest age of Italian music, we must concede that Mozart may have felt a little confined, a little bored, in the charming atmosphere of Salzburg.

Sigismund, the Archbishop of his childhood,

was dead, and a new Archbishop, Count Hieronymus von Colloredo, Bishop of Gurk, had been appointed. This personage has been much blamed, and it is beyond question that he was most difficult where Mozart was concerned ; but, even so, the circumstances were sufficiently extraordinary, for it transpires that, in a little tiny town like Salzburg, his predecessor, Sigismund, had nearly a hundred musicians attached to his Court—probably more musicians than there were soldiers. But Hieronymus, though he kept up his predecessor's establishment and was fond of music in his way, never made the most of Mozart. In fact, he was just as unpleasant to him as it was possible to be. It took the form of cancelling his leave to go abroad and insisting upon his writing works of minor importance and trivial character. This kept down Mozart's ceaseless output into certain channels, though nothing could ever interrupt his energy and fluency. Also, Mozart had, at least, the advantages of his own disadvantages. If his works had to be slight they possessed, at the same time, all the graces and elegancies of the Rococo age.

For four years, 1774 to 1778, Mozart wrote no symphonies, and, in opera, only La Finta

Giardiniera and Il Ré Pastore. Neither of
these is of particular merit. All his energies
were centred upon slighter and more ephemeral
forms ; but, before he had actually embarked
upon this phase, he composed a series of four
symphonies which in a curious way foreshadowed the developments of his mature
style. They are in a grave, serious manner
(K. 183, K. 200, K. 201, K. 202). There are,
also, a set of six string-quartets (K. 168-173),
and this form, again, he was not to touch any
more from 1773 to 1784. Having made these
various experiments in what he could do at
his best, he seems to have settled down for the
time being to a series of brilliant facilities. This
is the so-called ' gallant ' style, but perhaps the
Rococo style is a better way of expressing its
character.

With an artist of such prodigious energy,
and so open to every influence, it is next to
impossible to follow Mozart through all his
plethora of expression. He was growing hopeless over the conditions of his life, with the
petty conditions put upon him, and the small
opportunities open to him. But this affected
him in the way that, just because he was dis-
contented, although sure of his powers, he refused to go far below the surface. He was

disillusioned and thought little of his audience. So we find, in his music of this time, a trace of the young man isolated in the country who wants to be in the capital. There is a little of the sense of a straining, on his part, after fashionable effect. Perhaps no one except Mozart would have ever wholly recovered from this.

Nevertheless, during this difficult time, he wrote five violin concertos and the Haffner Serenade. This was in 1775 ; he was not yet twenty years old. All of these have the most enchanting Rococo spirit, and, probably just because he was so full of cares, they are of an entirely carefree character. The final movements, or rondeaux, are especially charming, and it is one more proof of his versatility that he used to perform the solo parts in these concertos himself.

The next two years were years of church-music, serenades, and divertimenti. The Archbishop was becoming more and more tiresome, and it is probable that there were domestic troubles as well. It can be seen from Wolfgang's letters to his sister that he was liable to fall in love at the slightest provocation. He had never been master of himself, for his father was incessantly with him, and the consequent lack of any self-reliance had a most weakening effect upon his character. Even if he could get leave to go abroad from the Archbishop, there was not a chance of his being allowed to go by himself. Leopold was planning another European tour for Wolfgang, but, when it came to the point, the absence of both father and son from their duties was impossible, and so Wolfgang had to set off with his mother.

The whole of the year 1778 was spent in travelling, and this was the last time that Mozart set foot outside the German-speaking world.

The mother and son spent some time at Mannheim. This was the capital of the Prince Palatine Karl Theodor, and under his influence it was one of the musical capitals of the world. They arrived there just in time, for a few months later Karl Theodor became Elector of Bavaria and went to live in Munich. The Mannheim orchestra had for years been the best in Germany. Some critics have taken a serious view about Karl Theodor, and he is accused of having kept an orchestra just because he wanted dancers for his harem and they had to have music before they could be, as it were, set in motion, but, however this may be, the Mannheim orchestra left a profound impression upon

Mozart. Also, perhaps, because these things were in the air at Mannheim, he had several love-affairs. There were certainly three of them : Rosa Cannabich, Augusta Wendling (a favourite of the Elector's), and Aloysia Weber. They were all singers or musicians.

The Weber family were to play a large part in Mozart's life. The father, Fridolin Weber, a music-copyist, was the uncle of the great Karl Maria von Weber. First of all Wolfgang was in love with Aloysia, but she refused him and made an unhappy marriage with a tragedian. So late as 1830, when asked by someone about her association with Mozart, all Aloysia would say was that she knew nothing of the greatness of his genius—she saw him only as a little man. After he had been rejected by her, Wolfgang made love to her younger sister Constanze, but the course of their love must be kept till a later page of this book.

Meanwhile, Wolfgang and his mother were in Paris. It was fifteen years since his portrait had been in the windows of the print-shops, and it was as though his life had begun all over again. He was remembered, but there was no curiosity about him. Grimm, who had been a sort of social sponsor to him when he came to Paris as a child, again took him into the salons.

The same thing happened time after time. He was kept waiting, and when he played every-one else talked ; but his situation in Paris could not be better described than in one of his own letters to his father. ' You advise me to visit a great deal,' he writes, ' in order to make new acquaintances, or to revive the old ones. That is, however, impossible. The distance is too great, and the ways too miry to go on foot; the muddy state of Paris being indescribable ; and to take a coach, one may soon drive away four or five livres, and all in vain, for the people merely pay you compliments and then it is over. They ask me to come on this or that day—I play, and then they say, " C'est un prodige, c'est incon-cevable, c'est étonnant " ; and then " à Dieu." '

But, in spite of this disappointment, a variety of new influences worked upon him, and so his visit was not without profit. All his ambitions were centred upon opera, and, at this time, the polite world of Paris was in a turmoil over the respective merits of Piccini and Gluck. Piccini it is impossible to discuss. There is hardly a living person who has heard a note of his music, and so we cannot tell if it deserved to perish. Probably it did not. Anyway, rightly or wrongly, it has been completely vanquished and crushed out of existence by Gluck.

At sixty years of age Gluck had suddenly
and completely changed his style. His new
operas were as revolutionary in their day as
those of Wagner, and he had produced four of
them, Iphigénie en Aulide, Orfeo, Alceste, and
Armide, in rapid succession in Paris. Gluck
was a wonderful master of sublime effect obtained by simple means. Grandeur, dignity,
purity, were his qualities. His curtains are
always wonderful instances of dramatic effect.
There is nothing of the eighteenth century in
his music, but it seems really to have come out
of an antique world.

That Mozart was profoundly affected, not to
say influenced, by Gluck can be seen in his
opera Idomeneo, produced two years later ;
but, meanwhile, three flute quartets, a couple
of concertos and an andante for the same instrument, are, as it were, miniatures of his studies of
Gluck. Side by side with these there are a
whole series of other works in which he has
set out to catch the French spirit. These are
violin sonatas, or piano sonatas, more particularly the famous A major sonata for the piano
with the Rondo alla Turca (K. 331). If this
delightful thing is to be compared visually
with any other work of art it would appear to
lie between some of Callot's engravings and

the chinoiseries of Gillot or Boucher. And it is doubly unfortunate that so little is heard of the music of Grétry or Philidor or Gossec, because in that we might find the solution of many mysteries concerning the changes of direction taken by Mozart at this time, more particularly in this decorated, ornamental phase of his.

In the middle of his stay in Paris he was offered the post of organist at Versailles, but he refused it. He was still in love with Aloysia Weber and could not bear the separation from her. Leopold wanted him to accept the post, and, had he done so, the whole course of his life, and therefore of music, would have been altered. But, without speculating upon such interesting possibilities, we must pass on to the death of his mother. She died towards the end of his stay in Paris, and he was alone for the first time in his life.

His hopes for a European, as opposed to a German, fame had vanished ; he had achieved but little success in Paris ; his mother was dead ; his break with Aloysia was close upon him ; and, worst of all, he had to go back to Salzburg. It was only natural that he should linger on the way as much as he could, stopping again at Mannheim and at Munich. It was

31

in this latter place that he quarrelled with Aloysia, and, in her default, made love to her younger sister, Constanze.

He got back to Salzburg in January 1779, and there were still two years and a half to go by before his final break with the Archbishop. During all this time, and in spite of all his frustrations, Mozart worked unceasingly as ever. The two operas Idomeneo and Il Seraglio date from this period, and out of the mass of his other work it is necessary to mention the Symphonie Concertante for violin and viola in E flat (K. 364). This is still frequently performed, and it does not fall short in any way of the very finest compositions of his mature years.

But, apart from that work, and from the two operas already mentioned, the rest of this two years and more was taken up with essentially Rococo compositions. He was without any hopes and only wanted to be gay and to amuse his audience and himself. His situation at the Archbishop's Court was one of inconceivable humiliation for a man of his genius. He was treated as inferior to the valets and had to wear the Archbishop's livery. This would have been hard enough to bear for anyone conscious of his talent, but for Mozart, who had been the wonder of half Europe, it was completely intolerable.

This ugliness in his own life had the effect of driving him into the utmost refinements of luxury in his music ; and luxury is usually a little superficial. His masses of this time are exactly comparable to the Rococo churches of Bavaria. Whoever has seen Kloster Ettal, or Ries, or Osterhofen, or Weltenburg, has had this phase of Mozart's genius translated into terms of the visual arts. The incredible delicacy of the melodic line, curling into itself like the tendrils of a vine, then shaking itself free and running on from support to support through all the architecture ; the bright thin flashing colours ; the clustered seraph heads ; the beautiful girls, dressed as angels, but showing the prettiest legs and arms through their ragged dresses, while they smile down on you from their clouds as from a sunlit balcony ; these delights of the Bavarian Rococo are all to be found in Mozart's church-music of this particular period.

These shades of gallantry are in his chamber-music too, in his sonatas, and in his serenades and divertimenti. That exquisite masterpiece, the pavilion of the Amalienberg, near Munich, is echoed in these. Its silver filigree, its mirrors, its delicate fancies of the frost are there ; and, like the Amalienberg, the melodies are so slight and tenuous that a breath would dissolve them.

It was the end of his youth. And now the miracle happened, for this extraordinary genius lifted himself out of all the minor elegancies of the Rococo age, and, having had a final quarrel with the Archbishop, left Salzburg and went to live in Vienna.

From now onwards his life was to be a series of tragic disappointments, but he was now the Mozart that we know. It was 1781 ; he was twenty-five years old, and for another ten years he was to enrich the world with the wonders of his art. There was no longer any question of his talent running into channels that were unworthy of it, for his genius flowered from the moment that he left Salzburg. His opportunity had come at last.

The amount and the diversity of his work were already so fabulous as to be scarcely credible. Perhaps there is no other artist, save Keats, who had attained to such heights at so early an age. Music came to him as easily as speech, and he must have written nearly as much as he spoke. But, at eighteen, when Keats started writing poetry, Mozart was already a veteran in his profession.

In spite of this, all the great Mozart lies before us. It is difficult to explain how an artist of such quick and prodigal gifts should have kept his speed and profusion of output while taking on a new depth and seriousness scarcely to be expected of someone with his temperament. This was a double miracle, more wonderful even than the marvels of his childhood, but its explanation is the influence of Haydn upon him. He took the quartet and the symphony from Haydn and made them his own. It was Haydn who started him in this direction, and he climbed to the full height of his powers along its paths.

The deepest influence upon Mozart's work came from Haydn ; but his younger brother, Michael Haydn, must be mentioned also. He passed all his long, dull life in Salzburg on a salary equivalent to some forty-eight pounds a year, and his numberless compositions, nearly unknown to us, were not without their effect upon Mozart. But, to Mozart, the greatest composer of the day was Haydn—and, to Haydn, it was Mozart. Neither composer had any doubts as to this.

III

THE VIENNESE PERIOD—1781-1788

As soon as he had left Salzburg Mozart married Constanze Weber. The next seven years saw the heights of his fame and the dashing of his hopes. These years were his maturity, and it is time, therefore, to speak a little of him as a physical being.

Probably everyone interested enough to open a book upon Mozart would know him from his portraits, but a diligent search through the likenesses taken of him in his lifetime leaves the impression that the best of them, indeed the only true one, is the portrait by Lange, the travelling-actor, in the Mozarteum at Salzburg. It dates from about 1782, the year after this chapter begins. It must reproduce, very accurately, the appearance of Mozart while he played the harpsichord.

The head is bowed, the eyes are fixed upon some near, but intangible, object floating in the air between himself and the keyboard. In fact, it is a picture of him, inspired, and, as such, though only an accurate likeness and not a work of art, this portrait is unique of its kind. There is nothing, in all the iconography of great men, to compare with it. The shape of his hair, his forehead, his look of youth, these are well shown ; and so are his mouth and chin, which, by themselves, are those of a musician. Indeed, from them alone it could be told that he was in the act of playing at his instrument.

I think it is easy to see his character from this picture. The long shaped head, with space in it for every technical resource and for the power of carrying the most complicated schemes of composition in the memory without having to note them down ; the poetical forehead, like the forehead of Keats ; these are true and re-markable properties of genius ; but there is something of the child still in him. You have only to see the lower part of his face to know of his inexperience in money matters and his weak-ness in affairs of the world. But how infinitely more subtle it is than the face of Beethoven ! There, physical awkwardness and a certain de-light in being misunderstood are expressed. Beethoven has, also, a look of brutal strength, and, because of that, he died at fifty-seven years

37

of age, older, by more than twenty years, than
Mozart. Twenty years more of Mozart, what
would that have meant, and it would scarcely
have carried him to middle-age !

Altogether, it is an extraordinary appearance,
extraordinary for its delicate genius ; but even
in this early portrait he looks ill. It is recorded
that he never had the penetrating eyes associated with genius ; they were dull and lifeless.
He was short-sighted from excessive application, and from the fatigue and illnesses of
childhood.

The Irish singer, Michael Kelly, who knew
him well, says of him, ' He was a remarkably
small man, very thin and pale, with a profusion
of fine fair hair, of which he was rather vain.'
He goes on to speak of his love of dancing.
Constanze Mozart used to say that, great as his
genius was, he was an enthusiast in dancing,
and often said that his tastes lay in that art,
rather than in music. We are told, elsewhere,
that he used to frequent the masqued balls of
the carnival in Vienna, and was actually incomparable as Pierrot or Harlequin.

It is in character, too, with his physiognomy,
that he should be a little lazy. Though it
seems a vain complaint against someone of his
fertility of output, nevertheless it is true that

38

Mozart never began any piece of music until the very last moment possible. He would continue playing bowls, or billiards, until it seemed too late to start. The results of this were an inordinate amount of night-work, very bad for his eyes, and for his health generally. He could write in the midst of a roomful of people talking, but when he played there had to be complete silence, or he would stop at once. This was the effect of his nerves, but also of his pride. He was vain, as well, about his clothes, and anxious not to be mistaken for someone of inferior position. Kelly, describing him during the first performance of Figaro, says, ' I remember Mozart was on the stage with his crimson pelisse and gold-laced cocked hat, giving the time of the music to the orchestra.' [1] These are traits belonging essentially to a person of small stature, and, a sentence or two later, Kelly describes the ' little man ' acknowledging the applause. But there was no more to it than these slight idiosyncrasies, for never was there a man of more simple and lovable character than Mozart.

Remarks about his entire absorption, while playing, are necessarily to be met with, and this is not remarkable in a man who must have been

[1] Gluck, Haydn, and Paesiello were in the house !

one of the most beautiful players imaginable. Whom would we have sooner heard, Chopin or Mozart? It is impossible to choose between them, but those who heard Mozart describe it as the experience of their lifetime.

It was, indeed, as a virtuoso upon the harpsichord that Mozart presented himself to the public of Vienna during the first four or five years that he lived there. For, at the beginning, he was too preoccupied with other things to give up his time to the major forms of composition. Much of his energy was taken up with the drudgery of giving music-lessons, one of the most signal instances of time wasted in the whole of musical history. At this period, nearly every forenoon was taken up with pupils, and he had to play at a concert nearly every evening. All through the spring of 1784, for instance, he played, on practically alternate nights, at the palaces of the Galitzin and Esterhazy families. An infinity of pieces for the piano were the natural outcome of his being so much in demand as a player. Indeed, with the exception of a single string-quartet, the whole of 1784 was spent by Mozart in teaching, composing for, and playing on the piano. It was, thus, that no less than eleven piano concertos date from the period immediately preceding

the production of Figaro. Many of these concertos he wrote for his own subscription concerts ; and then, as well, there were numerous
piano pieces, sonatas, fantasias, variations,
written for himself or his pupils, sometimes in
the form of duets. There was, also, his extempore playing, an art in which it is probable,
from the mere nature of his genius, that he
was never surpassed.

From this incessant and arduous salon-work
he achieved the highest reputation, but only
made the modest income of a music-master.
It was a course of things that could not continue, and he was drawn inevitably towards the
world of opera. But, in the meantime, he
finished the six Haydn quartets. This is not
the place to speak of them, but they are his
finest work of the kind ; they have been re-
garded, indeed, as the summit of all his musical
achievement.

The last two of these quartets were completed
early in 1785, and, after a few months marked
by almost as many piano concertos, and no
less than three months in the autumn with no
work whatever done in them, the year of the
Marriage of Figaro came. He was still only
thirty years old, was full of hope, and had none,
as yet, of the gloomy forebodings of death

which overshadowed his last years, and which seem to have been almost entirely the result of nervous prostration from overwork. On the contrary, it is probable that he felt himself to be on the threshold of a successful career.

Just at the right time he met the adventurer, Lorenzo da Ponte, a converted Jew, a priest, a character who might have been the twin-brother of Casanova—and it may be added, a most able librettist. Mozart suggested to him the subject of Beaumarchais' comedy, which had just been produced in Paris, and Da Ponte fell in with the idea and produced a book from it which is the absolute model of what comedy should be.

Apart from its beauty, which no words could describe, the Marriage of Figaro is of twofold importance. It set the model for all comic opera of the future. The Barber of Seville, Fledermaus, even Offenbach and Chabrier are foreshadowed in it. Besides that, it typified, as nothing else could have done, the civilization of which it was the outcome and the commentary. All political feeling, all the revolutionary moral, had been stripped from the play, and Mozart turned it, instead, into a mirror for all the finer feeling and fine manners of the time. A person who wanted to see the old world of Europe at its best, before it was touched by industrialism, and by America, need only hear the Marriage of Figaro.

Mozart made of Figaro the epitome of its day. It was essentially the matter of the hour ; its very excellence was because he was not bothering about posterity, or what they would think of it. He made living characters for the first time in opera, so that in the whole of it there is no single song that could be sung by anyone but the person for whom it was intended. The ensembles are wonders of characterization ; every air is a masterpiece of the purest poetry ; and yet the persons are as living as figures out of a novel, and they are imbued with a poetry that no work of fiction has ever possessed. ·

It would have been expecting too much of any age, or any public, for this opera to be an instantaneous success ; and, really, it profited Mozart very little indeed, but he went straight on from it, as was his custom, to other things— chamber-music, in this instance, for he was at work on two quartets. He was soon, though, to be the subject of popular acclamation on account of Figaro. This was in Prague, which he visited a few months later, in January 1787. He was received in Prague with real transports of enthusiasm ; a new opera, the unborn

Don Giovanni, was commissioned from him for performance in the winter, and, at one of his concerts, his exquisite Prague symphony in D (K. 504) was played for the first time.

About this time the project of settling in England was much in his mind. Michael Kelly and Nancy Storace, who had sung in Figaro, must have encouraged him in this, but it came to nothing partly because Leopold, now become an old man, refused to look after Wolfgang's two children while he was away. He may have felt that the time was not yet arrived for him to settle abroad, and he was pressed with work at home, more particularly with Don Giovanni, and with the two great string-quintets in C and G minor (K. 515 and K. 516).

But his mood was becoming anxious and strained. In April 1787 he writes to his father, ' Since death (take my words literally) is the true goal of our lives, I have made myself so well acquainted during the past two years with this true and best friend of mankind, that the idea of it has not only no more terror for me but much that is reassuring and consoling.' This is in an exaggerated tone, even when it is allowed that he was writing to a loved relation whom he knew to be not far from the point of death. In fact, Leopold died the following month, and it would be interesting to know what were his last thoughts about his son. His love for Wolfgang was of the most touching nature, but, as Holmes says in his *Life of Mozart*, Leopold had long since entered that poetical hell of Dante, which consists in ceasing to hope. It would certainly appear, from the letter quoted above, that Wolfgang had gone beyond its gates as well. He had no proper appointment, yet, no salary, and was crushed with overwork and the impossibility of making a proper living. The next thing was to be Constanze's illness.

Meanwhile Don Giovanni was produced at Prague, in the autumn, with tremendous success. It must have been like a revival of the fame of his youth ; but he could not get it performed in Vienna till May of the following year, 1788, and it did not please the Viennese public. However he had, in the meantime, been appointed Chamber-musician and Court composer by Joseph II., in the place of Gluck, who had just died. It brought him in a salary of about £80 a year, and his duties consisted in writing dances for the Court-balls—minuets, waltzes, and country-dances. The unfortunate thing about this post was that it prevented Mozart from leaving the country and going abroad to find his fortune ; he was kept in Vienna by a feeling of sentiment and loyalty for the Emperor. But his condition was just what it had been before, and there was no hope of improvement. His feelings about it can be guessed from the legend that, once, when he received his pay, he sent back a sealed receipt with the words, ' Too much for what I do—too little for what I could do.'

Before he descended into complete hopelessness, to the degree that he would not go to England though given the best inducements and the promise of a good salary, he seems to have made one more final effort. Even this was more in the nature of a proof to himself, once again, of his own powers than any sure bait for the public, for the three great symphonies that he now wrote were never performed in his lifetime, since the concerts for which they were intended never took place. These symphonies must be discussed elsewhere, but they marked the climax of Mozart's productivity. He had kept a careful list of his compositions, month by month, ever since February 1784, and, if we look at this, there is a marked diminution of his output after this time, after the autumn of 1788, that is to say. He had three more years to live, and he only composed about half as much as in the three years preceding this. Illness and debt defeated him.

This is a good opportunity, before that last and melancholy stage of his career, to try and sum up all that he had done since he arrived from Salzburg, full of hope, and in the conscious flowering of such a talent as hardly any other human being has ever possessed. In the short space of seven years he wrote, as we have seen, about twelve piano concertos; the six Haydn quartets; the quartet in D; three piano quartets; two string-quintets; five piano trios; five great symphonies; a mass of miscellaneous work including songs, sonatas, piano-pieces, divertimenti, and suites of dances; and three operatic masterpieces, Il Seraglio, Figaro, and Don Giovanni.

He had carried every branch of musical art to a higher pitch than it had yet reached. Piano concertos can be hardly said to have had an existence before he began writing his, and, in operas, the arts of ensemble-writing and of musical characterization appeared for the first time in the Marriage of Figaro. The string-quartet and the symphony he brought forward from the point at which Haydn had stopped, and Haydn, in his turn, became pupil to Mozart, and, under his influence, developed as

47

he could never have done if left to his own invention.

At the same time, except perhaps in the six Haydn quartets and in the three great final symphonies, there is a feeling in all he did that this was not much more than the beginning of his achievement, not much more than the improvisation of his vast talent. He was thirty-two years old at the age we leave him in this chapter, and what had Bach or Beethoven done, by then, to compare with him? Most unfortunately he was without their physical strength, their power of resistance. Also, as a child, he had known such notoriety as they never had, and he could never again settle down to life in humble circumstances. Haydn, with his peasant origin, was content with much smaller hopes, and then, where patronage was necessary, he had, in the service of Prince Ester-hazy, the most generous master, unlimited time, few worries, and an orchestra always at hand for his experiments. Mozart's temperament was, at once, his best quality and his downfall. Beethoven could not have written a single one of the letters penned by Mozart. None of them are heavy, none are sententious, none betray the slightest feeling of worry or disquiet about his processes of work. He had the gayest

48

and most mercurial nature, encouraged by the slightest turn of fortune, and, as easily, thrown into despair. It was only after unparalleled efforts in every way of music and an equal lack of response on the part of the public in answer to every one of them, that Mozart became hopeless. Then, he fell rapidly and with an impetus helped by every fresh and untoward circumstance.

An equal genius, working with greater care, could not have bettered the masterpieces he achieved in these years, for a great part of their quality is their ease and speed, their freshness and their spontaneous beauties. But this was only his youth, and he should have entered, at the end of this period, into a mood of more slow and considered things, into the maturity of his talent. There is no doubt that the best thing that could have happened to him was residence in England. It is beyond question that he would have made a proper income, for the English remembered Handel as their pride and welcomed Haydn with the true appreciation of his worth.

But all the maturity of Mozart is lost to us. There are only hints of it in his final work. His genius illumined everything he touched, but it had few opportunities, from now onwards.

D 49

Thus, in a sense, his life had its natural proportion, for he reached the apex of his achievement a little space of time before he died, and we get a sort of lull, after that, out of which his occasional utterances have an uncanny assurance and certainty. It is dreadful to think how easily this might have been remedied ; but, on the other hand, the thing to wonder at is that this extraordinary man ever survived his childhood.

IV

CHAMBER-MUSIC

WE, now, interrupt our narrative of Mozart's life in order to examine separately some phases of his work. He had written half a dozen quartets (K. 168-173) at Salzburg, in 1773, at sixteen years old, but he did not touch this form again till nine years later. Then, over a period of three years, between 1782 and 1785, he wrote the six Haydn quartets. The reason why they are called the Haydn quartets is because they were published with a dedication to Haydn ; and, if any more proof of their importance among Mozart's works is needed, it lies in his own words that they were the fruit of long and laborious effort. These quartets, with another odd one, and the set of three written to the order of the King of Prussia, form Mozart's quartets, so far as the musical public is concerned. There are, in fact, ten of them.

This makes a large number to choose among, and, in any case, Mozart's quartets are not to be

51

lightly approached. They have none of that
quality of delightful Arabesque, of ornament for
ornament's sake, which is the beauty of many
of his pianoforte sonatas. In them we are reminded of the most delicate Rococo decorations ; they may be like the finest stucco-work,
but their prettiness, grace, and rapidity make
us forgive them for being fashioned out of a
substance that is little better than sugar. They
have as well, a poetical, an Arcadian, simplicity.

Nor must we expect our ears to be ravished
by the harmonies of strange instruments, as in
the Serenades and Cassations. No composer
has ever understood the qualities of individual
instruments as did Mozart ; neither has anyone, except Mozart, had such power in impart-
ing a quality of ephemeral beauty, so that, in a
Serenade or Cassation, the impression is given
that this is the most beautiful little thing ever
heard and that it was only meant for a single
performance, and no more than that. This is,
indeed, one of the chief things about Mozart, for
his extraordinary care for detail made some of
his most seldom heard experiments into true
masterpieces of their kind. As for his drama-
tization of the qualities of the instruments it is
only necessary, in order to know this, to have
heard the oboe or the clarinet quartet, or one of

the concertos for French horn, or bassoon.
Mozart had the art of producing, in these, a
sort of pastoral or bucolic beauty, a poetry like
that of Theocritus, but with more humour ;
where the horn was concerned he put in
flourishes and distant hunting-calls, heard
through the trees, and blown by someone out
of breath with running; and, with the bassoon,
it is like a sea-god speaking, and the most
beautiful and elaborate fancies of Debussy, in
La Mer, are not more evocative of the spray, of
Neptune with his flashing trident, and of the
tritons sounding their conch-shells.

The quartets are more serious—in fact, they
are the most serious things he wrote, for he took
his time over the work and they have not that
element of inspired and divine improvisation
which is to be found in his symphonies—except-
ing always the Jupiter. He was writing them
to prove his power, to show every possibility
and every combination of the four voices in all
their range of emotions, and in order to demon-
strate his admiration for Haydn.

The art of quartet-writing had been developed out of all recognition by Haydn's
labours. Before him, it had been little better
than an excuse for polite conversation ; music
started the talking, and music had to go on in

order to cover up its traces. But Haydn lifted it on to an intellectual plane, and made it into one of the most wonderful vehicles ever invented for the statement of ideas and the embodying of poetical emotions. The amount of work done by Haydn in this medium can scarcely be credited, were it not that his achievement is equally stupendous in the matter of symphonies. He wrote no fewer than eighty-three quartets ; and perhaps the quickest way to understand what this means is to put it into terms of gramophone records, for his quartets would take up at least one hundred and sixty, double-sided, disks. Of these eighty-three quartets, at least forty or fifty are of equal, first-rate merit ; and, in this century, when the curiosity of the public is so easily and quickly appeased with photographs of all the good paintings and all the good buildings of the world, when their bulk can be reduced into a shelf or two of volumes, and when a few months of travel will serve to see them all in their different localities, the quartets of Haydn form about the greatest heap of untouched treasure still waiting discovery ; their importance, in this respect, being equal to that of the one hundred and four symphonies of Haydn, and to that of the one hundred and ninety Bach

54

cantatas, which, also, form a total from which it is so difficult to choose the best pieces that, in the end, the whole thing has been left practically virgin and untouched. But Bach is, at any rate, published and standardized, whereas the projected complete edition of Haydn's works is hardly more than half-way through its scope, and, for want of a proper and systematic catalogue, there is no right system of reference to Haydn's music; the opus numbers have never been properly arranged, and there is, therefore, always a certain amount of confusion where his works are concerned.

If Haydn was the precursor of Mozart, so far as quartet-writing was concerned, there must, naturally, in that vast output, be many points of difference, as well as of resemblance, between the two masters. Mozart was more serious and more ethereal. The peasant origin of Haydn, his Croatian ancestry, and his nearly Croatian environment at Esterhaza and at Eisenstadt, come out very clearly. The minuets, like the minuets of his symphonies, are true peasant dances. His was essentially the genius of hard work, and five hours of daily application had developed an ingenuity in him that reached almost to the heights of inspiration. The machinery, the carpentry, are marvellous, and his development of a second subject is often as neat as a conjuring trick. If his minuets are like the village-band, turned into poetry, his last movements are generally built up from a base of optimism and humour, and there is certainly sufficient ground in them to believe the legend as to his method of composition. For he is supposed to have found his inspiration in arranging objects on the writing-table, on the floor, or in the fireplace, in such a manner that they formed houses, or figures of persons, little miniature dramas, in fact, and out of these he found his themes and developed his atmosphere. He got his ideas from everyday domestic happenings, from the clop-trot of a horse's hooves, or the ticking of a clock, from the kitchen, the farm-yard, and the village-street. The result was liveliness, neatness, and the most delightful humour in the world.

Mozart, on the other hand, dealt either with the purely intellectual, the mathematical possibilities, or else played upon the moods and emotions. There is none of the homeliness of Haydn, and apart from his adoption of Haydn's formula of three or four movements for the quartet, and the similarity in general structure, the only mental resemblance, the only resemblance in attitude, is, again, in the minuets.

But, if Haydn gives the impression of, himself, joining in these peasant dances, or, at any rate, writing the music for them, Mozart is standing apart and giving his commentary on the scene. His attitude is like that of Watteau in the Fêtes Galantes ; he is an invisible spectator.

It is necessary, too, to draw a distinction between the quartets already published by Haydn and those written by him after close personal contact with Mozart, when he was, in his turn, influenced by him.

The first of these six quartets of Mozart, that in G major (K. 387), strikes a note of deep seriousness from its very beginning. There is a delightful minuet ; an andante of exquisite sensibility and grace ; and, for the last movement, a quick and lively fugue. The second of these quartets, in D minor (K. 421), is more beautiful still—is the most beautiful of all his quartets—but is of a piercing and appalling sadness. It is less formal, less contrapuntal in structure, and relies more upon sheer melodic beauty ; and, when Mozart did that, no one has ever excelled him. The first movement is of most romantic nature, using this word in the sense to which it applies to Schubert ; and it is certain that Mozart was in a highly emotional state when he wrote it, as it was during his wife's first confinement. The minuet, of inexpressible beauty, is of breath-taking sadness, as if the artist knew the fate that was in store for him and was thinking, while he wrote it, of all the times that he had ever been happy. The last movement, supposed to have been written by Mozart in a single night, during the critical hours when he was awaiting his son's birth, is a Sicilienne. It is one of the loveliest things he ever wrote, and hearing it is a pleasure only comparable to that yielded by reading the finest imaginable poetry. In fact, the senses are drugged by it, and the imagination can conceive of nothing more beautiful than this Sicilienne.

The third of the series, in E flat major (K. 428), is not quite on the same level. It is more gay and intimate in character. The minuet is wholly delightful. The fourth of the quartets, in B flat (K. 458), is that known as the Hunt quartet, because its first theme is like a hunting-call. The whole thing is incomparable for delicacy and neatness.

The final pair of quartets, that in A (K. 464) and that in C (K. 465), were written close on one another. The first of these has a slow movement in variation form. The whole quartet is serious in style and near the D minor

in mood. The second of these was begun only
four days after the completion of the other.
This quartet, owing to its stringencies, has
always come in for much discussion. It has
dissonances and false relations, which, at the
time, must have seemed of daring originality.
These occur particularly at the opening of the
first movement, but the quartet, as a whole, is
one of Mozart's most original and controversial
works, and, coming after the incredible sure-
ness of the others, and after their manifold and
exquisite beauties put into every musical form
possible, this quartet in C may be said to bring
the whole Haydn series to a stimulating end,
as though the composer wished to say how
many problems there were still to resolve
and what treasures he had not yet put into
spending.

He wrote one more quartet, in D (K. 499),
the following year, 1786. It is an isolated work,
completed not long after the Marriage of Figaro.
The Haydn quartets had not been, in any sense,
a popular success, and perhaps Mozart had
made up his mind for one more attempt, more
to please himself than the audience or the publishers, who, in the case of the firm of Artaria,
mistook some of his original ideas for mistakes
that he had overlooked. All the same this

quartet, for all its beauties, is not quite on the exalted plane of its six predecessors.

After this, his next string-quartets date from a period of his life that we have not yet reached. We shall see, when we come to resume our account of his career, that he was taken by Prince Lichnowsky to Berlin in the spring of 1789. He visited Frederick William II. at Potsdam, who was, himself, a good musician and played the 'cello. He received Mozart with enthusiasm and commissioned a set of six quartets from him, only three of which were ever completed. Although they were composed about the same time as Cosi fan Tutte there is little in them of the gay spirit of that opera. The first of them, in D major (K. 575), was written soon after his return from Berlin ; the other two, in B flat (K. 589) and F major (K. 590), a year later, in 1790. In all of them, because they were written specially for the King, there is considerable emphasis on the violoncello, and in one of them, at the royal request, he has introduced themes from Figaro and treated them in a curious and interesting way. Altogether, these quartets are strict, cold, and rather formal ; and it is, perhaps, safe to think that in writing them Mozart was in a stage of experiment, reaching out towards the

changes he would naturally have undergone
had he survived. The Haydn quartets were
statements of power ; these are more like works
of research, and when he wrote them Mozart
was nearly hopeless, but not yet in his last and
wonderful mood of creation.

Finally, in, as it were, appendix to his
quartets, there is the adagio and fugue for
quartet which he wrote in 1787, and which is
really a new version of a piece for piano duet
which he had written four years before. He,
also, about this time, set five of Bach's fugues,
from the Forty-Eight, for a quartet of strings.

During the years when he was so much in
demand at Vienna as a piano virtuoso, in the
time of the piano concertos, in fact, Mozart,
who never overlooked any form and was cease-
lessly experimenting, wrote a pair of piano
quartets, in which he doubtless, himself, took
the piano part. They are in G minor (K. 478)
and E flat (K. 493). The difference in his
writing for this combination and purely for
strings is an interesting study. The piano appears somewhat after the manner of a brilliant
conversationalist, but of that sort who far from
engaging in a monologue has the gift of making
his companions seem as amusing as himself.
The second of these two works, which was

written immediately after Figaro, is the better instance of this. The whole treatment is much less formal, and less passionate, than for string-work alone, and the effect is exactly that of the most delightful discussion, in, it may be added, a most beautiful room. The richness of invention, and the never-ceasing melodic inspiration, are as remarkable as the grace and good-humour of this enchanting thing. But his publishers refused to be associated with any further projects of the kind, and he never wrote any more for piano quartet.

In addition to his writings for quartets Mozart composed five quintets for strings. The quintet in B flat (K. 174) is an early work of 1773. Two quintets in C (K. 515) and in G minor (K. 516) were written in 1787, another in D (K. 593) in 1790, and a final one, in E flat (K. 614), in the last months of his life. A second viola has been added to the ordinary string-combination, and this, of itself, dictated the mood of the music to a certain extent. The quality of the viola is a kind of melancholy beauty, and no high spirits, therefore, are to be expected in these works. They were really a new experiment, on the part of Mozart, for even Haydn had not written for string-quintet.

The better of the earlier pair, that in G minor

(K. 516), is one of Mozart's most exquisite creations. It is a most scientifically constructed work, full of almost imperceptible allusions and harmonic devices. At the same time, to a first hearing, this consideration is quite subordinated to the haunting, sad poetry of the thing. The minuet is unforgettable ; and the last movement is a rondo which is so infinitely varied in form, and so magical in its variety, as to be the absolute culmination of one aspect of Mozart's talent. At moments there are the beginnings of the waltz in it ; and the apparent freedom of his imagination, over all that complicated substructure, all the hidden architecture, makes this rondo remarkable even in that world of wonders.

The last pair of quintets, written, as has been said, in the final year of his life, were composed to the request of a patron whose identity has never been discovered. ' At the earnest solicitation of a musical friend ' are the words written upon them. They are of great interest as showing the style towards which Mozart was moving when death overtook him. Although written with a few months' interval between them, they possess the same character and form a true pair. They are bold in style and most original in treatment. The first movement of the last quintet is built up from a single theme which is subjected to every conceivable device. The quintet is difficult to play and none too easy to understand, so that certainly, even if Mozart had lived, it would have escaped the attention that it deserved. At the same time it is written with the most extraordinary air of ease, very different from the atmosphere in which Beethoven wrote his best chamber-works. In them, in spite of their wonderful mastery, their mathematical certainty, the clearness of their exposition, there is always the consciousness of Beethoven's note-books and his incessant workings and strivings after perfection. Mozart had never to look for perfection ; he found it ready to his hand.

Since this is the last of Mozart's chamber-works it is, if only for that reason, of absorbing interest. The structure is formal and complicated, but illumined with those touches of apparent simplicity, which, with Mozart, have all the quality of divine utterance. The minuet of this quintet is of exceptional loveliness ; and the trio is a delicate, and, as it were, primitive waltz, throwing its shadow forward towards Schubert, or even Weber.

It is a pity that since the last quartets of Beethoven are often played, and have come to be acknowledged as almost the most interesting phase of his genius, these two final quintets by Mozart should be so seldom performed. His early death makes all the problems of his possible development of more moment than similar questions posed with regard to Beethoven, who had nearly a quarter of a century more of life in which to exercise his mastery. But, in spite of this, they are played on such rare occasions that it is nearly impossible to form any considered opinion upon them.

V

CONCERTOS

THIS is one of the most delightful of the forms in which Mozart's genius asserted itself. Freedom of imagination, neatness, and poetry could go no further. These things are apparent at the first hearing of a Mozart concerto, and deeper acquaintance with them leaves this impression unimpaired, while it discovers a much greater difference in style than would be thought possible when the quantity of his work in this direction is considered. Perhaps the reason for this is that his personal contact with the music was much closer than in, for instance, one of his own symphonies. In fact, he played the solo part in both his violin and pianoforte concertos, and his very evident personal fastidiousness made him as careful of the effect he produced as if it was a question of the suit of clothes he was wearing at the concert. Of course his own actual playing of the solo part was designed to show off his particular talents

66

of execution. We have, therefore, in the concertos Mozart, himself, as though these beautiful compositions were a set of frames for his own
portrait.

But they were much more than a mere
machinery of display for the instrument. Some
of them may be described as copious patterns of
decoration in the manner of the very finest
Rococo stucchi, but such comparative easiness
is only to be remarked in the least good of
them. In others of them there is work on his
very best level. There are pastoral, Arcadian
scenes of an indescribable poetry, and so apparently simple that they are the very breath of
inspiration itself. In some instances he has
given a military turn to the finale so that it has
all the stir and clang of martial music with the
colours of bright uniforms. Then, again, with
a flourish or two of the cor-de-chasse he evokes
all the romance of hunting in the autumn
woods ; the winding of horns through the trees,
the burnished leaves, even the early frost and
the bonfire-smoke. Other movements may be
more serious, like intellectual problems, set,
and solved of themselves with all the ease of a
successful card-trick. In the later of his concertos the atmosphere becomes grave and
solemn, charged with tragedy. On the lighter

side there are delightful moments like a brilliant conversation in a charming room ; and, to end with, there are often enough his rondos, which, alone, and in themselves, embody so many different forms of gaiety.

These rondos, or rondeaux as he wrote them, appear more particularly in his violin concertos. He wrote five of these in the one year 1775. He was then nineteen years old. These concertos belong to his Salzburg period, indeed, they are perhaps the best things he wrote at that time, and in the whole literature of the violin there is nothing so pleasant. No one else, saving Brahms, overcame the difficulties of this apparently simple and facile form. There is a most welcome absence in them of display for display's sake. Instead, the virtuosity is kept in check while beauty and poetry are allowed out in their place.

But, in his own time, these violin concertos met with a far from favourable reception. This is what Ditters von Dittersdorf, who is remembered more for his delightful journal, one of the best documents of the German age of Rococo, than as a musician, says of these very rondeaux that we are discussing. ' He gives his hearers no time to breathe : as soon as one beautiful idea is grasped, it is succeeded by

another, which drives the first from the mind :
and so it goes on, until at the end, not one of
these beauties remains in the memory.' His
words might be a criticism of modern poetry ;
and the interest of it is that it shows the dazz-
ling speed and brilliance with which Mozart
appeared to his contemporaries.

The rondeaux can be relied upon to be
delightful in their high spirits, and, as their
name implies, they are, perhaps, a little French
in atmosphere ; in fact, they are typical of
Mozart in his gallant manner, and gallantry,
at that time, could not be unaffected by the
reign of Louis xv. On the other hand, the
slow movements are always enchanting in their
delicate pleading.

It is easy to take all five concertos together,
because they form a whole and the same
atmosphere runs through them all. But the
three best of them are in G major (K. 216),
D major (K. 218), and A major (K. 219).
This last one, which is played, perhaps, more
often than the others, has a minuet movement of the most delicious nature, with a
Turkish episode for a middle section. It is a
little bit like the famous Rondo alla Turca of
the A major pianoforte sonata (K. 331), and
some of the effects are to be seen, in embryonic

form, of the Turkish music he was to write, a few years later, in Il Seraglio. These Turkish experiments are a kind of essay in chinoiserie, and they must be thought of with Boucher's Chinese tapestries. In fact they are a typically Rococo expedient, and the same train of ideas can be followed out in figures of Dresden porcelain and on delicately painted French tea-services and coffee-sets.

This particular concerto was his culmination in this manner, for the sixth violin concerto, written a couple of years later, is a work of minor importance. So is a seventh, the authenticity of which is questioned.

But one of Mozart's most beautiful achievements in this branch of the art still remains to be considered. This is his Symphonie Concertante for violin and viola and orchestra in E flat (K. 364), written in 1779. This is in the ordinary concert repertory of to-day, and is not infrequently played, when it always creates a deep impression. It is an isolated work, foreshadowing his more serious and mature style, and is, in this respect, a most extraordinary performance from so young a musician. The themes are unforgettably lovely, and if this exquisite thing can be heard played by Kreisler and Tertis the memory of it is ineffaceable.

This leaves the field clear for a discussion of Mozart's pianoforte concertos, and it is a region in which it is quite impossible to be disappointed. That is to say, any one of them is bound to be a delight to the ear, while the fact that there are no fewer than twenty-five of them makes it impossible for any number of the ordinary public to become satiated with them. And this astonishing number does not take account of four more concertos which are adaptations, by Mozart, of works by other composers ; nor of concertos by him for two and three pianofortes and orchestra. Of the twenty-five works more directly in question the author has heard a bare half-dozen, and his ignorance has had to be supplemented by reference to all the available published accounts of them. But it may be taken for a certainty, that, if all are delightful, at least a dozen of these pianoforte concertos are works of the very highest possible quality, are, in fact, undisputed masterpieces of their sort. It is, therefore, the more remarkable that they are so seldom performed, since more of the Mozart that the world loves lies concealed in them than in any other branch of his protean activity.

Some hint has already been given of their diversity of treatment and of the effects produced in them. Nearly all of them belong to his Viennese period, and, in particular, to those years during which he was so much in demand as a virtuoso. We may imagine them as being written in a few days, and, as always with Mozart, at the last possible moment, with some public subscription concert in view, or an approaching engagement to play in some private house. In this manner, in the period just preceding the Marriage of Figaro, he wrote no less than eleven concertos. They nearly all date from that time, from his period of optimism, and they naturally reflect its character.

It has been suggested that at least a dozen of these pianoforte concertos should be in the concert repertory, but these four of them, D minor (K. 466), C major (K. 467), C minor (K. 491), and C major (K. 503), are those most often performed. The first of them was a particular favourite with Ferruccio Busoni, who used to play it in inimitable manner with an exquisite cadenza of his own devising.

No musical experience could have been more beautiful than to have heard Mozart, himself, play the cadenza to one of his pianoforte concertos. The poetry and imagination, the quickness and delicacy of his execution, are gone for ever, but they must have formed a miracle of instantaneous invention, just as mysterious in origin as the finest poetical metaphors which spring apparently out of nothing. These, happily, are left on the printed page : but of Mozart's improvised playing nothing can be left. We may be certain, though, that poetical effect was his aim more than violence or brilliance.

Occasionally, in this Viennese period, he wrote concertos to be specially performed by some pupil of his. Those, for instance, in E flat (K. 482) and G major (K. 453), were composed for Barbara de Ployer. The first of them is delicate in mood and of exceptional finish and elegance ; the second is more symphonic in nature, and on a much fuller scale. It has a military finale, of glittering, scintillating effect. Mozart was very pleased with them, and they may have held an equal place in his esteem with that other pair which he wrote, at the same time, for his own concerts. It is in the latter of these that the finale, in rondo form, ends with a long crescendo of horns, as of a fanfare of huntsmen ; and it is said that this is not the only instance in which he has done this. Other concertos were written by Mozart for Mlle. Paradies and for Mlle. Jeunehomme, young Frenchwomen. They are, naturally,

French in style and treatment. Another pair of concertos, written in February 1785, are of special beauty. The first has an exceptionally gay rondo to finish with, and the second a finale of the utmost delicacy. It is supposed that Mozart played this before his father, on Leopold's last visit to Vienna ; Leopold, in his letters, describes these concerts at which he heard his beloved son for the last time on this earth, and the old man tells pathetically how the tears came into his eyes.

The pianoforte concertos seem to fall naturally into pairs. Such are the Coronation concertos, in F (K. 459) and D (537), so called because Mozart performed them at a concert in Frankfurt, in October 1790, during the Coronation festivities of the Emperor Leopold II. One of this pair of concertos has an andante so exquisite in nature as to defy any attempt at description. It is as simple, apparently, as a one-finger exercise.

After 1786, the year of Figaro, only two more concertos appeared. His phase as a virtuoso was over ; he was tired of taking pupils, and his mood was changing into the terrible despondency of his last months. These two concertos in question are in D (K. 537) and in B flat (K. 595). The latter was written in the spring of 1791, being one of his very last compositions. Both concertos are very different from the typical works of his Viennese period ; of far deeper solemnity and importance.

Finally, it is necessary to mention a concerto for three pianos (K. 242) and one for two pianos (K. 365). The former of these was written in 1776 for a Countess Lodron and her two daughters. The third part, but it is impossible to know for which of the trio it was destined, is of particularly simple nature. The most interesting thing about the concerto is that the cadenzas are written out in full, forming the only approach to any definite knowledge of Mozart's procedure about this. The latter concerto, that for two pianos, was composed in 1779 at Salzburg, and was written for Mozart himself, and for his sister. It is of brilliant character, and the final rondo is based on a popular French song.

The body of Mozart's music which is most accessible to the public consists of his sonatas for pianoforte, and for pianoforte and violin. At one time these were immensely popular, but now that musical amateurs of the sort are nearly extinct, owing to gramophone and wireless, it may be supposed that these works are much less familiar than they were a generation ago. There are, in all, thirty-two violin sonatas, and there is, naturally, much diversity of style among them. A group of six interesting sonatas are K. 55 to K. 60, written during the Italian tour of 1772, on Italian models, and under the influence of Corelli and Sammartini. These are the first instances in which he has made the violin and piano parts of equal importance, so that the violin is not merely obbligato, as in the sonatas of his childhood.

In this short space it is only possible to indicate which are the most famous of his violin sonatas. An excellent example is (K. 304), written at Paris ; and another good pair are those in E flat (K. 380) and in B flat major (K. 454). This last was written, at his best period, in 1784, for a splendid Italian violinist, Regina Strinasacchi of Mantua ; Mozart, himself, played the piano part, and the composition was so hurried that he played his part from memory, having had no time to write it down the evening before. Of the remainder of his violin sonatas those which are best known are in E flat (K. 481) and in A (K. 526), dating respectively from 1785 and 1787. In general, it may be said that these works are more delightful and pretty than solemn in character. In fact, they abound in tunes that would make the fortune of a good musical comedy, and that have, most certainly, been a help to the composer of Rosenkavalier.

When we come to Mozart's music for pianoforte alone it is manifestly beyond the limits of this work to give more than the very barest summary of his accomplishment, for, of sonatas alone, he wrote seventeen. Many of the early ones were written for the clavier, and, therefore, sound better on the harpsichord than on the pianoforte. Those composed after 1775 were written for the piano. Two of Mozart's own favourites, played often by him, were the sonatas (K. 279) and (K. 284). Another good one is (K. 310). Two specially fine sonatas are (K. 457) and (K. 576). The first of these was written for Frau von Trattnern, a pupil of his ; and the latter, for Princess Frederika of Prussia, in July 1789, after his visit to Berlin. It is called the Trumpet sonata, owing to its opening theme which is like a fanfare. It is necessary, also, to mention the sonata in A major (K. 331), of 1778, which has the famous Rondo alla Turca.

There are, of course, innumerable other piano works of varying merit, besides the sonatas. Delightful examples are the Ronda in B minor (K. 511), of 1789, and the Adagio (K. 540), of 1788. Then there is the unfinished suite (K. 399), of 1782, which is written in pure Handelian style. Of the four great fantasias, that in C (K. 394) has a fine Handelian fugue. It dates from 1782. The greatest of all four fantasias is that in C minor (K. 475). It is dedicated to the same Frau von Trattnern, and it is the greatest of all his works for pianoforte solo. Small things by him, of exquisite beauty, are too numerous to count ; but a particularly good example is the gigue (K. 574) written at Leipzig in the album of the Court-organist Engel, in 1789, on his return from Berlin.

Pianoforte variations afforded unlimited scope for the delicacies of his imagination. The best of these would appear to be those on ' Mio caro Adone ' (K. 180), of 1773, and those on ' Come un agnello ' (K. 460), of 1784, an especially good year for Mozart. The variations on the tune of ' Ah, vous dirai-je, Maman ' (K. 265) were written by him in Paris, in 1778, and they are famous. The variations upon ' La belle française ' ; upon ' Je suis Lindor,' an air from Dezède's Barber of Seville ; and upon ' Lison dormait,' from Julie by

Dezède, all date from this same time. Other good variations, dating from 1782, are a set of six on a theme out of an opera by Paesiello, and a set of eight on the march from the Mariages Samnites of Grétry. There is, also, a delightful set of pastoral variations ; while those on ' Ein weit ist das Herrlische Ding ' (K. 613), of 1791, are interesting from their date as being among the very latest products of his genius.

Last of all, two more groups of his pianoforte works must be considered. He wrote several sonatas for four hands. That in F (K. 497) is reputed to be one of the very finest works of Mozart. It was written in 1780 ; and another good one, of the following year, is that in C (K. 521). He, also, wrote some good works for two pianos. The best of these are said to be the sonata in D (K. 418), of 1771, and a magnificent Fugue in C minor (K. 426), com-posed in 1783. This was an experiment in the Northern German style. It is severely contrapuntal ; and must obviously have inte-rested the composer a good deal more than did many of his facile improvisations, for many of his piano compositions may be called that.

Speaking generally, where the piano works of Mozart are concerned, it might be suggested that the critics have taken an altogether too serious point of view with regard to them. The internal conflicts, the sublime prospects, the rugged cathedrals, of musical dictionaries are altogether out of place. Many of them might be more fitly described as exquisite and delicate embroideries, or decorations of the stucco sort, such as may be seen in German Rococo buildings, or of the Arabesque kind, honeycomb vault, stalactite and filigree, as practised by Andalucian Moors in their prime of fancy. There are, also, specimens, without number, of pastoral and Arcadian simplicities ; and tunes of popular character leading towards the ' ländler ' and street waltzes of Schubert.

But this does not apply to the four fantasias, or to his other noblest works. In them he attained to a hardness of form and a beauty of thought that are only comparable to the later piano sonatas of Beethoven. And, as it was Mozart, they have at the same time more poetry and a greater ease of expression.

VI

CHURCH-MUSIC

MOZART did not write a great deal of church-music. The enlightenment of the eighteenth century was beginning to shake the foundations of religion. Still, there is no doubt that he had a natural tendency to piety, and his official position at Salzburg, in the pay of the Archbishop, made it incumbent on him to compose masses, motets, litanies, and so forth, for his master. That his religious feelings were genuine is proved by his remark on hearing the news of the death of Voltaire. This was during his second visit to Paris, in 1782, when his mother was just dead. He wrote his father a sad letter about it, and refers, in the course of it, to that ' godless arch-rascal, Voltaire, who has died like a dog, like a beast ; that is his reward.' His meaning is that Voltaire never received the last rites of the Church as he lay dying. This censure of the dead philosopher shows the orthodox opinions of Mozart at a time of his life when it might be thought he would be particularly open to the new tenets of doubt and speculation that were in the air. It is true, though, that the letter was written in solemn circumstances, and to his own father.

Religious music was still an integral part of the art ; it was half of it, in fact ; and, taking this into consideration, it is perhaps remarkable that Mozart wrote no more of it than he did. It is idle to pretend that it did not interest him, because any and every form of music did that. Rather than this, it may be assumed that anything to do with the Church reminded him too much of his bondage at Salzburg.

But, curiously enough, his post as composer to an ecclesiastical dignitary forced him more into the direction of musical frivolity than of seriousness. The Archbishop favoured the light Italian style. The family of Colloredo were of Italian origin, and it would be expecting too much of this prelate to insist that he should have preferred the solemn style of Northern Germany. The Italian mode was in his blood ; and, moreover, there was a great deal to be said for it, even if it is allowed that perhaps his taste in this direction was not of the best.

Both his master's disposition and the restrictions that he imposed upon the young musician forced Mozart into the style of gallantry. The masses that he wrote during his early days at Salzburg are, therefore, predominantly in the Rococo manner. During his Italian travels Mozart had come under the serious, the contrapuntal authority of Padre Martini, but he had also heard the Venetian and the Neapolitan music. If these were frivolous they were also spirited and beautiful.

It is interesting to study their effect upon a learned mind like that of Dr. Burney. This is what he says of Naples in his ' Musical Tour.' ' It was at Naples only that I expected to have my ears gratified with every musical luxury and refinement that Italy could afford. My visits to other places were in the way of business, for the performance of a task that I had assigned myself ; but I came hither animated with the hope of pleasure. And what lover of music could be in the place which had produced the two Scarlattis, Leonardo Leo, Pergolese, Porpora, Farinelli, Jomelli, Piccini, Traetta, Sacchini, and innumerable others of the first eminence among composers and performers, both vocal and instrumental, without the most sanguine expectations ? . . . In the manner of their executing music there is, at

Naples, an energy and fire not to be met with elsewhere, perhaps, in the whole universe : it is so ardent as to border upon fury, and from this impetuosity of genius, it is common for Neapolitan composers, in a movement which begins in a mild and sober manner, to set the orchestra in a blaze before it is finished. Like high-bred horses, they are impatient of the rein, and eagerly accelerate their motion to the utmost of their speed, as Dr. Johnson says that Shakespeare, in tragedy, is always struggling for an occasion to be comic.'

Does not this passage throw new light upon a dead and forgotten world ? If this was true of Neapolitan music, the same taste was in favour in Rome and in Venice. The composers mentioned by Dr. Burney are, with the solitary exception of the younger Scarlatti, completely and entirely unknown to the modern public, but their music was the fashion of Mozart's youth. He must have heard much of it, and he could not have been deaf to its virtues. Italy was the home of his art, and church-music had occupied at least half the time of the best musical minds of his day.

It was only later in life that he came upon Handel and Bach, and he immediately appreciated their genius, which, in the case of Bach, appealed to all the mathematical side of his own talent. But, until this happened, and that was not till after he had left Salzburg and gone to seek his fortune in Vienna, his theories of church-music must have been in line with those of the Italian masters of the time.

What these ideals may have been it is easy to see after a visit to any of the churches at Salzburg. Three of these are early works by the great Fischer von Erlach, and the best of them, the University Church, though built a generation and more before Mozart's birth, is only so much additional proof of the universal Italian influence. The chief altar is rayed and clouded with white and gold in the manner invented by Bernini for St. Peter's, and two windows, a tall oblong and an oval above it, throw light down upon this drift of clouds that is broken with gilded sun-rays and has flights of angels coming through its intervals. These same principles of design and ornament are, as it were, the devotional material for all the religious music of the day. But Mozart is lighter still in spirit; not more frivolous, but more poetical and graceful. The exact counterpart to his effects is to be found in architectural works more strictly of his own time, and, of these, no better examples could be found

85

than in the two monastery churches of Osterhofen and Weltenburg. They are on the early
reaches of the Danube, near Regensburg ; an
easy day's journey from Salzburg. These are
about the most exquisite specimens of Rococo
churches in existence, and they are the master
works of the two brothers, Egid Quirin and
Cosmas Damian Asam. No lover of Mozart
can deny the truth of this analogy, or can afford
to neglect this visual experience.

Of course there were other influences not pre-
eminently Italian. There were the masses of
Haydn, but these are just as much in keeping
with contemporary architecture. Haydn was
in all and everything the preceptor of Mozart.
It was Mendelssohn who described Haydn's
masses as ' scandalously gay ' ; but then the
character of Haydn's music is that he was not
afraid of life. The Stabat Mater of Rossini is
a very different matter. It is possible to be
surprised by that, even at this time, but it is
difficult to see how a musician of the sensibility of Mendelssohn can have failed to appre-
ciate the actual devotional fervour implicit in
Haydn's gaiety and cheerfulness. And it must
be said here, in parenthesis, that the only
branch of music practised by Haydn in which
he was not excelled by Mozart was in this very

direction of church-music. Haydn wrote a more considerable body of it than did Mozart, and the level of it is consistently higher. Haydn's masses form the third part of his work, his quartets and symphonies being the other two parts of it, and this side of his talent, save for the Creation, is nearly unknown to us. But his masses may be heard, excellently performed, in the Capuchin church at Vienna ; and then there is no longer any doubt as to their beauty, as to the nearly equal achievement of Mozart, or as to the considerable backing of contemporary work, constructed after the same principles and aiming at the same beauties, which lay behind Mozart to fortify his church-music when it is condemned for levity and theatrical effect. He was working, during those early days at Salzburg, in the accepted style current at the time, and this has too many beautiful things to its credit for it to be condemned without a patient hearing of its claims. These are defended, it is sought to prove, by the best architecture of the day, which is a direct application of the same imagery, merely by transference, from the aural into the visual arts. Once that is acknowledged, it is no longer possible to deny the beauty of either the one or the other. Perhaps it may be possible to sum up in one paragraph the accepted ingredients, the imagery, to be found in churches of the date, and then we shall see if they do not tally with the music to which they were the setting.

Let us say, then, that it was an architecture of harmonious flowing line ; that its abstract ornament of scrolls and curves was of a graceful intricacy not surpassed, even, in the Alhambra or at Isfahan ; that the painted ceilings, belonging, we may say, to the school of Tiepolo, take the place, perhaps, of the marches, the overtures, the serenades, the incidental music ; and that sculptors, like Ignaz Gunther, are the embodiment in their art of the amatory airs and soli of this music, which, as well as describing, is directly addressed to, the angelic personages concerned. In fact, the solo airs are like love-songs ; and the seraphic choruses could have been inspired by the beauty of the carved angels. Furthermore, the shafts of light, the gilded sun-rays, are so many scale-passages, lovely in their airiness ; and the cloud-effects, arranged over the altar, have all the soaring and floating qualities that can be simulated in music.

The architecture, indeed, tallies completely with the music ; but, unfortunately, while

buildings of the kind are becoming more understood and appreciated by the public, the masses
of Haydn and Mozart meet with but little
enthusiasm. There are several reasons for this;
there is the realization that Bach, who was so
different in aim, was perhaps the greatest artist
ever produced in the Aryan world ; and there
is the fact that the Roman Church rightly
encourages the music of a better and more
primitive period. For it is necessary to say
again that this is the only branch of music in
which Mozart was not entirely pre-eminent.

The first of his Masses that it is necessary to
consider were written in 1774. The early part
of this year saw great activity on his part in
the writing of church-music. This was at Salzburg ; and later on in the year, at Munich, he
was called upon by the Elector to compose for
his private chapel a couple of short Masses and
an Offertory for four voices and orchestra. The
Masses are of no particular importance, but
the Offertory he seems to have been pleased
with, for he sent it on to Padre Martini, for his
opinion of it.

Two years later, still at Salzburg, he wrote a
Mass, some more Litanies for four voices and
orchestra, and a set of four church sonatas.
These are for string-orchestra and organ. It

is probable that they formed a series of six
pieces, of which two are now lost. Their character may be described as light and brilliant ;
and the same may be said of three more Masses
that he wrote in the autumn of the same year.
One of these is the Coronation Mass ; and all
of them are well described as in Court uniform.
In subsequent months he wrote two more
church sonatas ; another Mass, an Offertory,
and a Gradual. This last Mass in F (K. 192)
is said to recall the finest modes of the old Neapolitan school. The Credo from it is based
on the theme afterwards used for the finale of
the Jupiter symphony.

All these pieces were written in the intervals
of composing serenades, divertimenti, cassations, and so forth ; and the character of that
other side of his activity is reflected here. This
is the very epoch of that light and brilliant
church-music that we have been at pains to
excuse.

After this, there is a gap of a few months.
Mozart wrote no more religious music until he
had come back from Paris. When he started
to do so again he began with a church sonata
for organ and orchestra, and followed this up
with a big and important Mass. This is the
most characteristic of all his works of this

description. It is in the same style as before, but even intensified in gaiety and clarity; in fact, it could not be better described than in the words of M. de Curzon who says of it, ' Let us admire, in terms of the concert-room, the Kyrie with its symphony of oboe and strings; the sonorous, rustling richness of the Gloria; the Credo which is like an opera-finale in character; the Benedictus which is a little quartet from a comic opera; the Agnus Dei like a popular song; and the lively stretto which serves as finale to the whole work.' This music fits as closely into a church of the time as do Figaro or Cosi fan Tutte into the delicate Rococo of the Residenz Theatre of Munich. A church, such as those already mentioned, or, to name another instance, the chapel of the monastery at Melk, is the most perfect setting for this Mass. And, as if the theatrical atmosphere was not already predominant, there are regular opera-boxes at Melk to hold the choir-singers.

There was, again, an interval of a few months, and then, in 1782, as a thank-offering for his marriage, Mozart composed the unfinished Great Mass in C minor (K. 427). This is his highest achievement in church-music, except for the Requiem. Now, for the first

time, there is a profound difference in atmosphere.   The Rococo element has nearly gone,
and, instead of it, there are the signs of his
intensive study of the old North German music.
The Mass is for four solo voices, chorus, organ,
and orchestra.   The most beautiful use is made
of the wind-instruments, especially in the Agnus
Dei, sung by a soprano voice to the accompaniment of organ, oboe, and bassoons.   The
whole thing is full of lovely moments, more
particularly the Cum sancto spiritu, a slow
fugue of basses, bassoons, and bass-trombones ;
and the Hosannah, which has some extraordinary effects of trombones as they work out
their separate parts in the fugue.   But the Mass
was unfinished, and it had to be edited in recent
years, and completed by adaptation from other
works of his, before a complete and satisfactory
performance became possible.

Various other, minor, religious works date
from these same months ; and then there come
nearly ten years with nothing more of the kind.
It was only in his last months that his religious
interests revived.   The sign of this renewal is
the Motet, Ave Verum Corpus (K. 618), which
he wrote for the choir-master Stoll, at Baden,
near Vienna.   Stoll had been kind to Constanze
Mozart, during a long convalescence from her

illness, and the Motet was a present from Mozart in appreciation of this. It is for four voices, organ, and string-quartet. The music is of the most moving simplicity and purity ; these qualities, indeed, have resulted in its being almost the only religious music by Mozart which is constantly and continually performed.

Finally there is the Requiem. Its mysterious and romantic history will be described when we come to talk of the last year of Mozart's life on earth. Here, it is only sought to give some indication of its character and atmosphere. The whole question of the Requiem is beset with difficulty and confusion. The Requiem consists of twelve numbers, of which only the two first have an actual existence in Mozart's handwriting. The remainder were completed by Süssmayer ; but there exist sketches by the master for six more of the movements, so that only four of them were entirely the work of Süssmayer. Of the remainder, apart from the two which were wholly by Mozart, the existent sketches by him were certainly sufficient ground for Süssmayer to proceed upon. He was such an intimate friend that his personality must have been saturated by Mozart's principles ; and, as well as that, he had heard the work incessantly discussed by Mozart during his last

93

illness, and must have had full knowledge of Mozart's intentions had he, himself, lived to complete the work. On the whole, therefore, far from blaming Süssmayer, full credit should be given him for making possible, as no one save someone in his exceptional position could have done, this expression of Mozart's last living feeling.

It has all the characteristics of final utterance about it. Not that the music is essentially of a tragical nature, but its effect is peculiar and nearly distorted in sentiment ; tortured sweetness ; long-drawn suffering ; all the terrors of death without too confident a note of belief ; a terror weighed down with doubt, and with no complacency or resignation about it ; these are its messages, and by no stressing of the imagination can they be said to be comforting.

His nerves, but not his creative powers, were nearly finished when he wrote it ; and this is what makes the Requiem so different from anything else. Like every other composition of Mozart, it was hurried : but hurried, this time, from other reasons. It is concerned not with a summing up of the experiences of life, a death-bed panorama ; nor with a picture of the blessed in the regions of eternity, which would have meant to Mozart an Arcadia, a pastoral paradise ; but its subject is more simply the experience of dying. It is a farewell, and the sadness of this music consists in the agony of separation. We understand enough of Mozart's character to know what were the things he would miss the most. In nearly every letter that he wrote there is the breath of his affections. The poetry of his music is in its human emotions transcendentalized. The Requiem is like a last survey of their pleasures and pains.

VII

SYMPHONIES

ANY appreciation of Mozart's symphonies is spoiled and disappointed by the thought of his early death. He had written, by the time he died, enough chamber-music, enough concertos, enough serenades and divertimenti. These he carried to their ultimate perfection ; and, in a sense, no more of them is needed, for he had time to achieve these forms in their finality. This is not so in his symphonies. If we except the Jupiter, it may be said that there is no other instance of his putting his full powers into activity. This was a period into which he had not yet entered. Had he lived, and there is no doubt that Mozart died just on the threshold of fortune, symphonies would have been commissioned from him in series, in sets of half a dozen and a dozen. He was to have visited England on the invitation of Salomon, to whom we owe the twelve Salomon symphonies of Haydn. A contract similar to this would have been offered to Mozart; and other engagements came to him, just before he died, from Prague, from Hungary, and from Holland. There is every reason to suppose that he would have abandoned, for some time, composition in minor musical forms in order to concentrate his energies upon the symphony and the opera. But in the latter, again, Mozart had already written masterpieces upon which even he could hardly improve. We must conclude, then, that our greatest loss from his death was in symphonic music.

Even so, not less than forty-one symphonies are to his credit, but, of these, not more than six or seven need enter into our discussion. The others are juvenile works of no particular importance. There is nothing to be discovered in them, as there is in neglected symphonies by Haydn. These are forgotten because there are so many of them. Probably forty or fifty of Haydn's symphonies are first-rate, but there is no room for them in the concert-repertory, and only a very few of them are ever given.

As Haydn had most influence upon Mozart some attempt must be made to contrast the two masters, for Mozart worked along the lines practised by the older man. His mature symphonies were written over a period of some forty years, ending after Mozart's death, and occupying in their entirety a longer span of time than Mozart's whole life. Haydn was as regular and industrious a worker as there could be, and the result was one hundred, and more, symphonies. When these are fairly judged on their merits, it will be found that his finest masterpieces in symphony are not inferior to those of Mozart. This is not surprising when it is considered how much more time he had.

If music is loved for its more simple and pure qualities, unmixed with introspection and self-analysis, free from egoism and self-pity, then the best of Haydn's symphonies are as beautiful as anything that the civilization of Europe has given us. Their clean, neat workmanship ; the manner in which, as in the Clock symphony, the simplest things of life are taken up and charged with humour and poetry ; the grace and liveliness of his minuets ; the speed and brilliance of his finales ; these are their qualities, and the expectation of them is never disappointed.

Mozart is more delicate, less earthly. The perfection of beauty is to be found in his andante. He has, there, an angelic, a seraphic tranquillity ; a peace in which, as it were, you would hear Haydn breathe. But in the minuet and trio Haydn is always predominant. In the hands of Mozart the minuet is very often the subject of a kind of courtly and aristocratic sadness ; with Haydn it is a true dance which touches the blood. The trio grows out of it, into the beginning, sometimes, of a Ländler or Viennese waltz. It has vigour and force, and strong pictorial power, so that a scene is evoked and the tune is remembered as much for that as for the particularities of its treatment. When the minuet comes back again, after the trio, it is with the grateful comfort of music heard once more that might have been gone for ever.

The reason for these differences between Mozart and Haydn lies to a great extent in a physical contrast, for physical things are too seldom taken into account in art-criticism. Mozart's music is always that of a small, pale, delicate man. Haydn is much more robust ; with a healthy unstrained childhood behind him, and with all the promise and accomplishment of old age before him. There are, therefore, qualities of ripeness and maturity in him that it would be naturally impossible for Mozart to possess. Another thing is that Haydn, safe in his position with the Esterhazy family, was never pressed for money. His music is, on this account alone, less nervous, less apprehensive than that of Mozart whose life was entirely wrecked from financial difficulty.

The quality of humour, as apart from wit, is not found in the symphonies of Mozart. The finales of the Haffner, or of the Symphony in C (K. 338), are models of speed and wit, but they are not amusing in the sense that Haydn was amusing. Nor has he ever the rustic simplicity of Haydn, whose minuets are often no more nor less than peasant dances to the village-band. Mozart, in fact, had more courtly manners. He had spent his childhood in playing at Royal Courts and in the houses of the great, and, as a young man, he had been under the necessity of composing an infinite number of pieces for table-music, to be played between the courses at banquets. Something of this early environment persisted in, at any rate, the earlier of his symphonies. It was this that made Wagner say of them, ' On myself, at least, the perpetually recurring and noisily garrulous half-closes of the Mozart symphony make an impression as if I were hearing the clatter of a prince's plates and dishes set to music.'

His richness and speed of invention being his most miraculous quality, it may seem superfluous to charge Mozart with having composed

his symphonies too quickly. His method of
composing is luckily preserved to us in his own
words, in one of his letters, and this swiftness
of fancy is explained there as the result of long
inward meditation. He carried his compositions already written, in his head ; but this
does not preclude their having been, as it were
improvised, by the amazing mechanism of his
mind. Saving, always, the Jupiter symphony, it might be argued that, still a young
man when he died, Mozart had so far written
little that he expected to last for long. His
operas, his concertos, his symphonies, everything that he wrote, he was ready to replace
with new ones at a moment's notice. This
may have been from full and justifiable con-
fidence in his own powers. He probably felt
that good fortune must come to him eventually
and that, then, he would have more time.

The earliest of his symphonies that it is necessary to mention is that in C (K. 338). This
was written at Salzburg in 1780. It has no
minuet, but this shortness of length is made up
for by an andante, longer than usual, and of
incredible beauty. The variety of invention is
astonishing, and it gives proof of such subtlety
of temperament, such poetical imagination,
as would be impossible of anyone else but

Mozart. And, like poetry, it is a distilment of the fancy more than the result of reasoned thinking. By no other method can the beauties of that andante be explained, save that it evolved out of itself by poetical method, by instinctive inspiration. It has, also, that atmosphere of affection which is a characteristic of Mozart, and which reminds us of the letters describing his childhood where we are told that he was for ever asking his family if they loved him. This craving for human affection, in order to have affection to give back, is implicit in the atmosphere of this lovely thing. And the andante is followed by a delightful finale, absolutely free of all care and worry and sparkling with high spirits. It is all too short ; like a run through the air on a snowy day, and the sound of it does really warm the body.

Two of Mozart's most exquisite masterpieces date from 1782 and the following year. These are the Haffner symphony, in D (K. 385), and the Linz, in C (K. 425). Both symphonies are on a small scale, and somewhat similar in treatment and atmosphere, so that, though written at an interval of a year, it is reasonable to think of them as a pair. The history of the Haffner is that it is taken from a serenade written for his friend Haffner at

Salzburg; but the serenade in question was not the same as the celebrated Haffner serenade. Mozart would seem to have been particularly pleased with the serenade that he should have remembered it months later and turned it into a symphony. The slow movement, as always, is the most beautiful of all and still shows its original conception as a serenade. It is absolutely appropriate for such an occasion ; and, in order to explain our meaning, we can do no better than quote what our hero's biographer, Edward Holmes, has to say of Mozart's serenades. 'These Sunday garden fêtes in the spring and early summer are peculiarly characteristic of life in Vienna, where the pleasures of the promenade, and the enjoyment of the air and sunshine, regularly succeed the observances of religion. In such a scene, where all the beauty, rank, and talent of the capital are assembled, the spirit of the season is irresistible. And there is the music. An orchestra is erected in some green walk among the trees ; and the first sound is the signal to suspend conversation, to sit down quietly, or to cluster round the musicians. . . . A style of instrumental music at once light and ariose—somewhat between the symphony and the dance, but calculated to give elegance and tenderness of sentiment to the promenaders—was at any time attractive to Mozart, and among his easiest work. His serenades were not such as the starved lover sings, but imbued with all the genius of the South ; in fact, when we consider the emotions aroused by Mozart's instrumental music, and by the adagios of his symphonies in particular, the imagination of the author may be compared to a Mahommedan paradise ; for in no other element can such refined voluptuousness and elegant repose be conceived to originate.'

Such is the exact character of the andante, and no one who has heard a performance of it under Toscanini will ever forget it. It is emphatically music for the open air, for the evening of a fine day ; and the allegro which follows is even more exhilarating than that of the symphony previously described. The spirits of Mozart never rose higher than in this finale.

The Linz symphony is, if not less beautiful, even slighter and more tenuous in structure. It was written while Mozart broke his journey from Salzburg to Vienna, and the whole matter, from the start of the work to its performance, was an affair of four days. It is laid out for a small orchestra and is practically a chamber-work ; but this apparent easiness and slightness conceals the greatest difficulties, for no work by Mozart is more subtle and delicate in its demands upon the players.

The next symphony written by Mozart was the Prague, in D (K. 504). It dates from 1786, the year of the Marriage of Figaro, when the genius of the composer was at its fullest flower. The result is one of the most beautiful things in the history of art. On this occasion, Mozart is much more deep and profound than in the pair of little and exquisite works that preceded it. The occasion was one of much importance to him, for it was played during his visit to the Bohemian capital, where Figaro was being performed with such triumphant success that a new opera, the future Don Giovanni, had been commissioned from him. Figaro had been a comparative failure in Vienna, so that, in Prague, Mozart was in the most congenial surroundings possible to him and felt called upon to produce the very best of which he was capable. As usual, it was dashed off with the greatest possible speed, and some of its most beautiful effects, in the long chain of melodies that form the andante, more especially, are clearly the results of afterthought, of last moment inspiration, while the ink on the page was still wet under his eyes. This andante is, perhaps, more touching and moving to the sentiments than anything else ever written by him. Its second subject is redolent of regret and affection and has an extraordinary moment like the opening of a pair of arms, a sort of sudden expansion of love. There is no minuet; and the finale is not of that order of brilliance as usually practised by him, but is, again, of beautiful, but melancholy character. This symphony, at its first performance, must have drawn tears from many eyes that had forgotten it a few moments later, but Mozart probably never expected to hear it played again.

After this, we come to the apex of Mozart's achievement, to the three immortal symphonies of 1788. The time was propitious; Don Giovanni had just been performed, his powers were at their highest. But troubles over money and worries of every description were crowding in upon him from every hand. His position was becoming hopeless, but, before he entered on his last phase, a period, for Mozart, of comparative inactivity, followed by a last and final spurt of energy, he produced these three masterpieces out of the superfluity of his talents, which could not, it would seem, find sufficient outlet for their tumultuous force. The three symphonies are entirely different in style, and were written by him in little more than six weeks. The concerts for which they were composed never took place, which fact was probably no surprise to Mozart in his dispirited condition, and they form, therefore, a wholly gratuitous display of his powers, written as much to satisfy himself as to please an audience.

The first of them is that in E flat (K. 543). So far as purity of melody is concerned, Mozart never wrote anything to excel this, and it is like a late epitomization of the style of gallantry of his youth. It has that Italian atmosphere brought back by Mozart from his travels, which we find in Figaro, in Cosi fan Tutte, and in the Serenade from Don Giovanni. Wagner may well have been thinking of this symphony when he wrote, ' Though the Italian operatic melody had kept to its threadbare formal build, it had received in the mouth of talented and feeling singers, and borne on the breath of the noblest musical organ, a graceful sensuous colouring as yet unknown to German musicians—a colouring whose euphony was absent from their instrumental melodies. It was Mozart who became aware of this charm, and, while he brought to Italian opera the richer development of the German mode of instrumental composition, he imparted in turn to the orchestral melody the full euphony of

107

the Italian mode of song.' There could be
no better explanation of the peculiar beauty of
this symphony.

The next one, in G minor (K. 550), is of entirely different character, and depicts another
world altogether. At the beginning it is melancholy, but the minuet and the finale are more
cheerful in mood. The atmosphere, though,
is not Italian. There is not that same warmth
and ease, that gallantry of the hot south which
no other artist has ever expressed so well in
any of the arts. This is no longer the Mozart
of Figaro ; it is more like the Mozart of the
Haydn quartets.

The final symphony, in C major (K. 551), is
the famous Jupiter. This is a masterpiece on
the purest lines of classical architecture, en-
riched with all the devices and ornaments of
polyphony. It is an expression of abstract, or
absolute beauty, deriving its effect from the
mathematical certainty and precision of its
parts. The fugal treatment of the final allegro
is without any parallel in music. Mozart dis-
plays, in this, his complete mastery of the
complicated forms of the Northern German
school, and in his effortless way he surpasses all
their achievement. If the wonderful fugue with
which Beethoven ends the Third Rasumoffsky

quartet is, perhaps, a little the same in spirit and in intention as this finale to the Jupiter, it is hardly necessary to stress the difference between a piece laid out for a quartet of strings and a movement employing all the resources of a large orchestra. It is of unique interest as being the only instance, in Mozart's symphonic music, of his attempting anything which put his powers of invention to a strong test, as opposed to the ordinary flowing of his unrivalled store of melody and poetry.

If this last movement is a triumphant ending to one phase of Mozart's genius, it is, also, an occasion for the utmost sadness. He lived for another three years, after the completion of this symphony, without ever returning to this form of music. But, had he survived, it may be concluded with certainty that the symphony would have been the instrument of his greatest successes. Had he lived only another twenty-three years, and died at Beethoven's age, the world would now be spurning half the music it accepts.

VIII

OPERAS

THE invention of Mozart in opera was characterization. His discoveries in that respect are comparable to the improvements brought into fiction by the psychological method of Dostoieffsky. In his mature operas it would be impossible to transport any air, or song, from one character to another, just as the slightest passing remark in the work of the Russian novelist is wholly indicative of the character from whose lips it issues. But while Mozart, like Dostoieffsky, was in this a master of narrative, he had also those sublime powers of poetry for which there is no room, or reason, in a Russian novel. And not only were his single airs the absolute property of his characters but he was, also, the first composer to treat ensemble singing on the same principles, so that the same tune could be varied in an infinite degree to suit each member of the ensemble. Wagner must have been thinking of this when he wrote of him, ' How deeply I love Mozart because he could not invent for Titus music like that for Don Giovanni.' Perhaps his powers of characterization are to be found at their best in Figaro, which is the most complete and satisfactory of all Mozart's operas. There is never an idle moment in that, while Don Giovanni, for all its beauty, is not on the same level, and it is too long. Figaro is too short : it could not go on long enough, and that is the difference between them.

The deepest of Mozart's ambitions, and the surest of his gifts, was for opera. Verdi, even in his old age, could never have made the Magic Flute, with its puerile fancies, into a supreme work of art. But Mozart achieved it through his excessive powers of poetry, which, in comparison with him, might almost be said to have been denied to every other operatic composer. Indeed, after having seen an opera by Mozart, the successive turns of ill-fortune undergone by this art-form since his death would seem to be on a par with the degradation of the piano concerto which blossomed in his hands into so many forms of beauty, and, ever since then, has been made into an excuse for bombast and the trivialities of virtuosity.

But it would be a mistake to over-estimate

Mozart's achievement in opera. There is no use in pretending that those of his operas which are never performed are any great loss to the public. This is certainly the case with Rossini, but it is not so with Mozart. There may be a good overture, a charming suite of ballet-dances, as in Idomeneo ; or one or two fine airs, but all his accomplishment is in the operas that everyone can hear, and there is no necessity to go beyond Il Seraglio, Figaro, Don Giovanni, Cosi fan Tutte, and the Magic Flute.

In these five operas there is all the range of human emotions, so that a preference expressed for any one of them must depend entirely upon personal taste. If I like Figaro most, other people will advance the claims of Don Giovanni or the Magic Flute. But certainly Figaro had the advantage of an admirable libretto, which offered Mozart all the opportunities he could wish for, and the opera exhibits Mozart's powers at their simplest and purest, even if it is argued that Mozart, himself, was equally happy in all these operas.

When he wrote Il Seraglio he was busily engaged in courting Constanze Weber, his future wife. The state of being in love had certainly its traditional effect of inspiration upon him in this lovely work, but the worries inseparable from that condition were also present, and, besides that, he had to deal with an unusually difficult and intricate libretto. Then, as well, the singers were always quarrelling, and one of the most important characters in the opera, the Pasha Selim, could only be given a speaking part because no suitable singer was available to fill the rôle. In addition, as always, the music had to be composed at breakneck speed, and, on top of that, the final production was delayed for a whole year. In fact, the circumstances were wholly uncongenial to the creation of a satisfactory work of art.

But Il Seraglio, in spite of this, has survived —for several reasons. First of all, the plot, in spite of its many drawbacks and handicaps, has a delightful, inconsequential humour of which Mozart has made the most. The Turkish music has the same spirit as the Rondo alla Turca and the Turkish episode in the A major violin concerto. It is conceived, that is to say, as a kind of chinoiserie, in the style that Gluck had invented for the forgotten opera, Les Pélerins de Mecque. Mozart's knowledge of this opera is proved by the set of pianoforte variations that he wrote on one of its airs. But there are other things, beside its quaintness, that have made Il Seraglio outlive, for instance, Idomeneo. In its most beautiful moments, the music has, certainly, that strange and piercing conviction, that impassioned utterance, we should expect of Mozart in the mood he was living in at the date of its composition. This is found in the duets of the lover Belmonte and the heroine Constanze, who was, doubtless, given that name at Mozart's instigation. But it occurs most of all in the serenade of Pedrillo. This is one of the most exquisite moments in all Mozart's creation. It is so beautiful as to defy any attempt at description or explanation ; but it belongs to that Italian world, that idealized Italian atmosphere in which Mozart dwelt at times. In spite of a few other beautiful airs this level is never reached again in the opera, but, as a whole, it can be characterized as a delightful entertainment with occasional passages of rare poetry. It is interesting to compare Il Seraglio with L'Italiana in Algeri, an early opera by Rossini, in which his amazing melodic gift is scattered far and wide with reckless generosity. L'Italiana in Algeri has nothing to equal Pedrillo's serenade, but the plot is more amusing and better made, the tunes are delightful beyond words, and the whole effect is like a glass, or several glasses of champagne. It was written thirty years after Il Seraglio, but is a real pendant to it, in the sense in which the Barber of Seville and Figaro must for ever remain linked to each other.

If we proceed straight from Il Seraglio to Don Giovanni, in defiance of chronology, and in order to keep Figaro, our favourite, till last, it is chiefly because the mention of Pedrillo's serenade carries the mind on to the serenade in Don Giovanni. 'Deh! Vieni alla finestra' could be made the subject of a whole dissertation upon the polish and elegance of manners, the blue skies of gallantry, and upon the Latin ethics of seduction. All the romantic aspects of the Renaissance civilization of Spain and Italy are summed up in that one, apparently simple air, which we may be sure came from Mozart without trouble and without forethought. And the minuet played from the window in the ball-room scene is another epitome, as entire as that in its understanding.

As the play proceeds, its original design as a comic opera is heightened and dignified into tragedy. This process is accompanied by a most wonderful flowering of beautiful airs, typical of which is the immortal 'Batti, batti, bel Musetto.' The duet, 'la ci darem,' is another of the miracles that no words can describe, and that only Mozart has ever had the power to create. By the time the banquet scene has been reached, and the element of the supernatural has come into the opera, we are living in a world that only Shakespeare, except Mozart, could make for us. Each time this scene is played it constitutes, in itself, one of the most romantic episodes in the whole of human history.

This is Mozart in all the wonders of his powers, but the Magic Flute is no less portentous in its display of his genius, for he has made a kind of fairy charivari into a vehicle for the most profound and touching emotions. The deepest mysteries of life and death are found growing out of this spectacular pantomime, for that is all it is, without Mozart. This has been accomplished by the intercalation of Masonic philosophy, in which Mozart was a neophyte, and by which he had been so profoundly affected that it had come, almost, to take the place of religion for him. It can be seen in Mozart's letters to what a degree he was influenced by it and how deeply his thoughts were turned to death and, in a sort, consoled, by Masonic doctrine.

The solemnities of the Magic Flute are, then, its prevailing character, but, also, and as an integral part of the scheme and not merely as an extraneous incident, there are the comic interludes for Papageno. For these, Mozart has invented music of a fanciful delicacy that seems to emanate from another world, it is so light and airy. The song of the Queen of the Night is another audacity of invention which conceals its extraordinary properties under the most wonderful flower of poetry. It appears to have been created at one jet, like a bird's song, and yet it is as artificial as the Isola Bella. Another wonderful moment is the song sung by two armoured men to Tamino. Bassoons, oboes and flutes accompany them in a tremendous display of counterpoint over an old German chorale, of Luther's time.

One of the most effective features of the Magic Flute is the use Mozart made of the deeper wind-instruments, more especially the trombones. They give character to the overture, and produce wonderful and awe-inspiring effects of solemnity in Sarastro's song, ' O Isis and Osiris.' They form, in fact, the Masonic background of the Magic Flute and signify the mysteries of its ritual. Through their use, the opera is lifted on to a mystical plane that puts it apart from any other work of Mozart. But it is, surely, a mistake to argue that because of

this aloofness, this independent stature, the
Magic Flute represents the true Mozart, in the
ultimate direction towards which he was moving
at the time of his death. The Masonic texture
of the opera is unequivocally the affair just of
the year or two in which it was written. It was
essentially of the epoch of the French Revolu-
tion. If the Magic Flute is typical of a year
or two of history, Figaro is the summing up of
a century and more. It must also be considered that, had he lived, the probabilities are
that within six months he would have been at
work on some opera diametrically different in
every respect from the Magic Flute. The
opera was a phase, made important by his
genius, but in no way representative of the final
trend of his thought. At the most, he would
have expected twenty or thirty performances
of it, and, by that time, would have been at
work on something new.

Figaro was written under the same conditions of speed, and for the same short-lived
hopes, but, because it was meant to typify the
moment and because it had no mystical intention, it penetrated so deep into ordinary, everyday life that it became life itself. The able,
unscrupulous hands of the librettist, Lorenzo
da Ponte, transformed Beaumarchais' play and

worked it into the most perfect example of an opera-book that there has ever been. Precisely its satire, its foreshadowing of the French political upheaval, was left out of the opera, till it became, indeed, not a reflection of the misdeeds of the rich, but a convincing argument of their virtues.

The Italian atmosphere is predominant, with all the mellifluous graces that Mozart had heard in Italy and had transposed and heightened in his fancy. This is the Italy with centuries of architecture and centuries of music behind it, falling, even then, into decay, but still an Arcadia for the eyes and ears. This scene Mozart has made to emanate from his characters by a kind of distillation of their sentiments, so that it is all implicit in their songs. It is the background of their emotions. Mozart's ambition must have been to provide the greatest possible momentary pleasure to the senses, and when he wrote Figaro he was not worrying about the distant future of his reputation. He was only letting all the beauties of his imagination find shape. His own pleasure in life entered into every phrase of the music, and the southern warmth was in his mind. What he created will have cost him little or no effort.

Figaro is, also, the Italian language put to its finest uses. This is apparent the moment the opera is heard played in German, in English, or, as I have heard it, in Swedish. In the last of these languages, in spite of a wholly admirable performance, the loss of the Italian tongue was remarkable to an almost pathetic degree. This is because the grace and simplicity of Italian match so admirably with those same qualities in the music.

The recitative, too, is one of the wonders of the opera. Its cadences seem to make a solid atmosphere round the characters, so that, when Figaro or Don Bartolo speak, the notes of the harpsichord are like pieces of furniture close to their elbow, or the corner of a stone building rising just behind them. If Figaro is played without the recitative a great part of its beauty is lost, for the effect of it is to give dignity and grace to every phrase, and the illusion is produced that the characters lived in a world of such attenuated luxury and refinement that the principles of the *haute école* entered into every commonplace detail of their existences.

The artificial nature of such a world as that is corrected by the simplicity and purity of the airs. And here the wonder of the thing really begins, because, by these apparently easy means, the characters are given individuality and life. By the end of the first scene this miracle has been accomplished, and, during the second scene, as the intrigue unfolds, there is that lovely running ensemble, which continues for some quarter of an hour or twenty minutes and appears in a hundred different guises adapted to the successive complexities of the plot and to the different characters in their respective sentiments and attitudes towards it. This is, perhaps, the best thing in the opera. Never, for a moment, is it confused or heavy : all is light and clear as day.

As a sample of Mozart's gift of swift characterization there is nothing better than the gardener's song when he bursts into the Countess's boudoir with his tale of broken flower-pots and the flying shade of Cherubino. Another moment of wonderful poetry is the exit of Figaro singing a snatch of his own air, ' Se vuol ballare, signor Contino,' to the accompaniment of a few notes played pizzicato. It is like the mockery of a serenade. It has a momentary, instantaneous poetry, like a beam of sunlight coming through an open door. Then there is that lovely, Arcadian strain of music to which the peasants, the contadini, appear before they are granted their holiday for Figaro's wedding. Few things in the world are as lovely as this ; but there is no use in trying to explain how or why it is achieved. It is the simplest, the easiest of strains, wreathed round with a sort of fluttering or descending ornamentation of the violins which suggests the garlands of flowers that the peasants are carrying. Close upon this follows Figaro's wedding-march, and it epitomizes all the pride of Gothick descent and all the fine manners and pomp of aristocracy. No more effective piece of stage-music has ever been written. It unfolds itself from no distance at all, gets nearer and closer, spreads and swells itself, and reaches to a fine climax of splendour out of nowhere. There is also the fandango, appropriately pompous and solemn and Spanish.

The best of the single airs out of Figaro it is impossible to analyse or dissect. If anything in the world is sacred, they are sacred. ' Voi che sapete,' ' Non so più cosa son, cosa faccio,' ' Deh ! Vieni non tardar,' ' Venite, inginoc-chiatevi,' what is the use in mentioning more than their mere names ? And, most lovely of all, the exquisite duet, ' Quel soave zeffiretto.' Nothing could be more beautiful than that, but how it started, or why it means what it does, is as mysterious as the process by which the Eve of St. Agnes was written.

If we have, now, to leave Figaro, it is in order to say a few words about Cosi fan Tutte. The plot of this opera is not nearly as bad as it is made out to be, and on the very rare occasions when it is given the opera makes a wholly delightful and harmonious impression. Its high speed and reckless gaiety appear, straight away, in the overture, which is surely the most perfect example of an overture to a comic opera, with its curious effects as of distant laughter. There is a world of difference between Cosi fan Tutte and Figaro. There are no fine sentiments in Cosi fan Tutte, and its purpose is only to amuse.

It was composed even quicker than usual, and then Mozart was finished with it. He never saw it again, or returned to it with any new airs or improvements. But his nerves, almost on the point of collapse, were at such a fine degree of energy and sensibility that the brilliance and sparkle of the music are unsurpassed. The ensemble writing is even more advanced than in Figaro. In the first scene a quintet, and then a sextet, are miraculous instances of this ; while, all through, there are airs and duets, which if they are cynical in intention, are no less beautiful in workmanship than those in Figaro. The duets of the two young girls, the songs of Guglielmo and Dorabella, of Fiordiligi and Ferrando, these are the other delights of Cosi fan Tutte. The opera is something apart in Mozart's creation ; and listening to it is like an hour or two of life, lived apart in a summer evening, that will go on for ever and that everyone has forgotten about.

IX

THE LAST YEARS—1788-1791

WE left off our account of Mozart's life at the close of the year 1788, and, before we enter into detail about his last three years of existence, we may sum up the extent of his achievement until this date. He had already written Figaro and Don Giovanni, six Haydn quartets, and all his symphonies. In the lesser forms of music his output had been so varied, but of such consistent excellence, that it is difficult to credit the true account of it in quantity, or quality. He was still only thirty-two years of age; and many great composers have produced little, or nothing, of value by that time of life.

But the shades were closing in on him. It was not only the disappointment of all his hopes of profit or preferment, but, also, he had acute money worries in the shape of debts, and was constrained to borrow money in order to pay his daily expenses. His chief creditor, in this respect, was Puchberg, a rich merchant.

Towards the end of this year, in response to a request for two thousand florins, Puchberg lent Mozart two hundred, and, a week or two later, Mozart had to write confessing his inability to pay this back and demanding still further advances. It was the beginning of grave troubles.

His next musical task was the rescoring of Handel. This was done to the demand of Baron van Swieten, a musical patron who deserved well of the world because he introduced the works of Handel and Bach to Mozart, gave the subjects of The Creation and The Seasons to Haydn, and was a friend to Beethoven. In this, and the following, year Mozart rearranged and gave additional parts to The Messiah, Acis and Galatea, Alexander's Feast, and The Ode for St. Cecilia's Day. It was work which has not been accorded an altogether favourable reception by lovers of Handel.

But a diversion of a new and perhaps more pleasant kind occurred in the course of it, for he was invited to go to Berlin by Prince Karl Lichnowsky, a patron who, again, in his turn was to befriend Beethoven. It meant travelling in luxury, and was a holiday for Mozart. They went to Berlin by way of Prague, Leipzig and Dresden, and were soon at Potsdam, where Mozart was received by Frederick William II.

and played to him. The King was a good player on the violoncello and commissioned a set of six string-quartets, while his daughter, Princess Frederika, ordered a set of pianoforte sonatas. The three quartets, described in a previous chapter, were the result of this ; and all Princess Frederika obtained from him was the so-called Trumpet sonata, in D major (K. 576). Soon afterwards he was back at Vienna, in worse financial straits than before, and having to make incessant appeals to Puchberg.

A period was now beginning in which Mozart, owing to worry and hopelessness, produced very little music. This continued for some eighteen months, and the final calamity was the illness of his wife, Constanze. She sank into being an invalid, and Mozart, who could never find intellectual companionship in her, because it was not there, was now saddled with all the expense of an invalid wife who had to be sent off to Baden, near Vienna, for a treatment of baths, and who, when she was with him, must have exhausted all his energy and vitality.

The effects of this were beginning to tell, even upon his character. While it is impossible to believe that he was ever a drunkard, it is true, nevertheless, that he frequently drank more than was good for him. Also, in his disillusionment, and with an ill wife, he began to have intrigues. While he was in Berlin there is no doubt that he had a love-affair with an actress called Henrietta Baranius, who was a mistress of the King's. It is futile to deny this, as does his biographer, because of the devoted tone of Mozart's letters to his wife during his absence from her. But no lover of Mozart can grudge him this last warming of his blood : for soon he was to lie cold in his grave.

Between his return from Berlin, and the end of 1789, he wrote little or nothing. The only exception is one of his most lovely works, the clarinet quintet in A (K. 581). Then there came Cosi fan Tutte, produced in January 1790 ; and, up to the end of that year, he wrote nothing except the two last of the trio of quartets written for the King of Prussia. The rescoring of Handel was his only other task. Such an inactivity had never happened before in his career. It is proof that things were going very wrong with him ; though, what few things he did accomplish, the two quartets, Cosi fan Tutte, and the clarinet concerto, were of exceptional beauty.

A new expedient for fortune offered itself to him in the autumn of 1790. The occasion was the coronation of Leopold ii. at Frankfurt, the

traditional crowning-place of the Holy Roman
Emperors. But, in order to get there, Mozart
had to borrow eight hundred florins from a
money-lender and pawn some of poor Constanze's few valuables. There is, indeed, something a little exaggerated and mysterious about
this sudden plunge into poverty, and, in his
letters, Mozart shows a kind of apologetic con-
trition which hints at there being some secret
cause for it of which we are ignorant, and of
which Constanze was ignorant too.

He took with him to Frankfurt, at his expense,
his brother-in-law, Hofer, the violinist. This
was typical of Mozart's generous nature, and
its effect was to preclude any conceivable hope
of profit. The visit ended in nothing. Mozart
played a pair of concertos, the ' Coronation '
concertos, at Frankfurt, and after a short stay
there proceeded to Offenbach, in order to
interview the music-publisher, André. Nothing
came of this either. André would not take
his manuscripts ; though, after his death, he
paid Constanze the equivalent of five hundred
pounds for them. Then he returned to Vienna
by way of Schwetzingen and Mannheim, a
visit which must have brought him sad re-
membrances of the hopes and happiness of his
youth. He arrived at Vienna in November,

I   129

in time to borrow a further two thousand florins.

But he had entered his last year of life, and he began, now, to fulfil the promises he had written to Constanze during his absence from her. ' I will work—work so hard—so that no unforeseen accident shall ever reduce us to such desperate straits again. What a delicious life will we lead ! ' he had written to her. The first sign of this renewal of creative energy was the magnificent string-quintet of December, in D major (K. 593). This was followed up, in April, by its companion in E flat (K. 614), and both were written, as has been indicated in the chapter dealing with his string-music, to the order of an unknown patron.

Another sign of his determination to work as hard as possible was his reappearance on the concert platform with a new pianoforte concerto, in B flat (K. 595). This was composed in January 1791, and was the last that he wrote, being separated by an interval of some years from the rest of that series of wonderful and varied masterpieces. It is grave and solemn, the work of an older man, but, as always, impeccable in style and grace.

During these last few months Mozart composed some pieces of novel and peculiar character, slight in intention, but raised by these late flickerings of his genius into an importance far above the purpose for which they were destined. The commission for them came from Count Deym's art-gallery, and, odd as this sounds, the details were more odd still. Some new improvements had lately been practised in the manufacture of musical-boxes. A toothed cylinder was made to revolve through the prongs of a fork, or comb, as is still the way with Swiss musical-boxes ; and for these, and for a chiming-clock that worked on the same principles, he produced several little works.

His letters mention the difficulty he had in driving himself on to complete this labour, but nothing he did when his nerves were so strained and his faculties at such a high level, was unworthy of him.

The results were two little masterpieces (K. 594), and the Fantasia in F minor (K. 608). The first is in the style of Handel. The second, in the style of Bach and influenced by the fugues and motets he had heard for the first time during his recent visit to Northern Germany, is in the form of an allegro between two adagios. Luckily it has been possible to preserve these in the form of duets for four hands ; and the writer remembers a superb performance of this latter piece by Busoni and his pupil, Egon Petri.   Later on, he wrote two more little pieces, a little movement for a clock, and an andante to a waltz for a little organ.   But these were not for Count Deym's country-house ; the order came from a jeweller or clock-maker.

Mention must be made, also, for it belongs to the same class of works, of a quintet for glass-harmonica, oboe, flute, viola, and violoncello (K. 617).   This was written for a blind girl, Marianne Kirchgässner, who was a talented performer on the glass-harmonica.   Judging by the level of his work at this time, and by the understanding that Mozart always possessed for the timbre of different instruments, there is every reason to think that this must be a most beautiful work.   It is in three movements, in the accepted quintet style.   There is, also, another work, a little adagio, that he wrote for glass-harmonica, probably for the same performer. Perhaps some day a musician from a country-fair, a clown, or another blind girl, will learn these forgotten pieces and appear with them before the public !   But the influence of these unusual compositions can be found in things universally known ; in, for example, the song of Papageno to glockenspiel accompaniment in the Magic Flute.   It is a moment of truly ravishing loveliness, and so may be the quintet for glass-harmonica !

At this time Mozart was writing an incredible profusion of dances for the Carnival. During the end of January and the beginning of February he delivered, for full orchestra, six minuets, six allemandes, four more minuets, four allemandes and two counterdances ; then, again, two minuets and two allemandes, six slow waltzes or ländler, a counterdance, six counterdances, and an allemande. The ländler must be particularly interesting ; and, of the rest, the trio of the last of the three Deutsches Tänze (K. 605) is the well-known ' Schlittenfahrt,' the dance with post-horns and sleigh-bells in the orchestra.

The end of his labours is coming nearer. In a more serious sphere of work he wrote a final chorus for an opera, ' Le Gelosie Villani,' by Sarti ; his beautiful ' Ave verum corpus,' and, probably, an ' Adoramus ' for four voices, bass, and organ. Then the Magic Flute took up his energies. In the midst of this, for his ruffianly friend Stadler, he wrote the beautiful clarinet concerto in A (K. 622). This is one of the very finest of his works, and a place must be found for a discussion of it at a further page of this work.

The Magic Flute was produced in Vienna, in September ; and, a week or two before that, another opera, La Clemenza di Tito, was given for the first time in Prague. It is a stiff, classical subject, to a libretto by Metastasio, but the theme was empty and old-fashioned, and Mozart cannot have felt much interest in it. He wrote an overture and twenty-six numbers for it, so that it is sure to contain interesting things, but Clemenza di Tito has never held the stage as the Magic Flute has done.

He wrote nothing else, save the Requiem, but the circumstances of this were so peculiar that they demand a detailed account. First of all, it is necessary to lay stress upon the appalling nerve-strain under which Mozart must have been labouring at the time, from money worries, from family troubles, and from an absolutely incessant production. He was in an exaggerated, hysterical state, the sort of condition which ends in serious nervous prostration, or in blood-poisoning.

At the worst time of this a particular thing happened that was, of all things, most calculated to make the trouble worse, and to bring on a crisis. ' A tall grave-looking man, dressed from head to foot in grey, and calculated from his very appearance to make a striking and

weird impression, presented Mozart with an
anonymous letter begging him, with many
flattering allusions to his accomplishments as
an artist, to name his price for composing a
Requiem, and the shortest time in which he
could undertake to complete it.' These are
the words of Otto Jahn, Mozart's biographer,
and it would be difficult to describe the strange-
ness of this visit in better terms. Nothing more
than that seems to have struck Mozart at the
moment, for he accepted the offer and set to
work at once.

But he was at breaking-point, and just this
additional commission, on top of the two operas
already in hand, brought on the crisis from
which he was never to recover. His press of
work was appalling; he had only a fortnight
in which to compose Clemenza di Tito, and
the Magic Flute was in hand as well. At the
beginning of September, as he was leaving his
house to start off on the journey to Prague,
where the first-named opera was produced, the
mysterious stranger again made his appearance
and asked how the Requiem was proceeding.
This second visitation had a fearful effect upon
Mozart, and he became obsessed by the idea
that the stranger was from the next world and
that the Requiem was to celebrate his own

death. It would seem, almost, as if his mental balance was upset. The idea was for ever in his mind, and he felt that his days were doomed.

A letter that he wrote to Lorenzo da Ponte, at this time, is a dreadful proof of his extreme mental tension. It is an expression of anguished nerves, and no one who loves Mozart can read it without being deeply affected by its pathos. ' I wish I could follow your advice, but how can I do so?' the letter runs. ' I feel stunned, I reason with difficulty, and I cannot rid myself of the vision of this unknown man. I see him perpetually; he entreats me, presses me, and impatiently demands the work. I go on writing, because composing tires me less than resting. Otherwise, I have nothing more to fear. I know from what I suffer that the hour is come; I am at the point of death; I have come to an end before having had the enjoyment of my talent. Life was, indeed, so beautiful, my career began under such fortunate auspices; but one cannot change one's own destiny. No one can measure his own days, one must resign oneself, it will be as providence wills, and so I finish my death-song; I must not leave it incomplete.'

The poor thing was broken and finished by the time this letter was written. A few days later Constanze came back from Baden to look after him. His latest letters to her were full of a pretence of hopefulness, and had little or no mention of his own condition of health, but it is safe to suppose that Constanze must have been told by friends that he was ill and peculiar in his ideas. When she had come back he took to his bed, and sank rapidly into a hopeless state. He had just strength enough to compose one more work, a little cantata (K. 623), for the opening of a lodge of Freemasons. He dragged himself out of bed to conduct this and then went back to it, never to rise again.

His mind was now delusioned, and he explained away his illness as an attempt by enemies to poison him. He still talked of his Requiem, telling Süssmayer how he wished it written ; and on evenings when the Magic Flute was performed he would look at his watch and think to himself of the opera. Some of the singers from the theatre came to see him. He asked for the score of the Requiem, and they sang parts of it to him until they reached the Lachrymosa, where he had a fit of weeping and they had to put the score away.

It was his last day on earth. His sister-in-law went in to see him and he called to her, ' You must stay to-night and see me die. The

taste of death is already on my tongue : I
taste death.' Yet they never sent for the
priests : perhaps his Masonic interests had
spoiled his faith. A last act of kindness was
typical of him. He asked Constanze to keep
his death secret from everyone save his friend
Albrechtsberger, that he might be the first to
apply for the vacant post of Kapellmeister at
St. Stephen's. He asked to look at the Requiem
again, and the doctor, entering, put cold appli-
cations to his head. He shuddered violently,
fell into delirium, remained in that state for
two hours, and at midnight died. It was the
fifth of December 1791. He would have been
thirty-six in two months' time.

His funeral was the next day. No one
troubled to give him expensive burial, and, as
it rained violently, the few friends who were
there hurried home. The coffin was put hastily
in a pauper's grave and covered over. A few
weeks later all trace of it had been lost among
the coffins of the other paupers ; and, to this
day, the body has never been found.

Thus died perhaps the most gifted human
being that has ever been born. It was death's
most dreadful achievement. Other artists,
Keats or Shelley, have died even younger ;
but, perhaps, if they had lived, there was not

so much more to come from them, and, in any case, they wrote in a single language and not in a universal tongue. The only loss to humanity that can compare with this came thirty-seven years later, and, also, in Vienna. This was Schubert. His case was as bad as that of Mozart, but Mozart had achieved more, and, in his own words, 'Life had been so beautiful'; his career had begun under such fortunate auspices. He was, as he truly said, taken away before he had the enjoyment of his talent. He was so near to it : and died just on its threshold. But even this much could not be said of Schubert !

X

CHARACTER OF MOZART

THE mystery about the Requiem must now be cleared up. The sinister stranger was no visitor from a supernatural world, but a certain Leutgeb, steward to Count Franz von Walsegg of Ruppach. The Count was in the habit of commissioning works from composers of more or less renown, which he performed in his own house and passed off to his friends as being of his own authorship. In this instance his wife had just died, and so a Requiem was opportune. The negotiations had to be conducted in mystery, and had Mozart been in good health his sentiment would have probably been one of amusement at the strange circumstances and the cloaked stranger.

It was in order to claim the full hundred ducats payment for the work that Constanze urged Süssmayer to complete the Requiem. And, having been paid this, Constanze got but little more from her dead husband's estate.

However, by the proceeds of some concerts she paid off his debts in full ; and, after some years of widowhood, married von Nissen, an Aulic counsellor to the King of Denmark. She lived many years in Copenhagen, and then returned to Salzburg, where she died in 1842, having, in spite of her delicate health, survived Mozart by more than half a century. There were two surviving children, both completely undistinguished, and the longest lived of them died in Milan, so late as 1859.

Meanwhile there was one more survivor, the ' Nannerl ' of Mozart's childhood, his sister Maria Anna. Many years before she had married Berchtold von Sonnenburg, a Baron of the Holy Roman Empire.

This is how she was living at Salzburg in 1829. 'We found Madame Sonnenburg, lodged in a small but clean room, bedridden and quite blind. Her's is a complete decay of nature ; suffering no pain, she lies like one awaiting the stroke of death, and will probably expire in her sleep. . . . Her voice was scarcely above a whisper, so that I was forced to lean my face close to her's to catch the sound. In the sitting-room still remained the old clavichord, on which the brother and sister had frequently played duets together ; and on its desk were some pieces of his composition, which were the last things his sister had played over previous to her illness.' Death came to her in the spring of the following year, after the writer of these words, Mrs. Novello, had raised a small subscription in England to give some comforts to her in her last year of life. This was how Mozart's beloved sister died, who had played the harpsichord with him in Paris and in London nearly seventy years before, when the future was full of promise for them both.

It is now time to say something about the character of the extraordinary being with whom these pages are occupied. There is luckily a great and, as it were, self-confessed source of information in the letters of Mozart and his father, Leopold. It is an extremely voluminous correspondence, and although Constanze destroyed on her husband's death all letters written to him by Leopold after the year 1782, because of the Masonic references which shocked her susceptibilities, there are, still, enough letters left to fill four volumes of five hundred pages each. The bulk of these are from Leopold, and it is interesting to note the gradual change in his attitude towards his son.

They begin in a tone of delighted amusement. He writes to friends about the little boy whom he looked upon as a plaything, a little clown, ' The latest thing is that. . . . Do but picture to yourself. . . . God daily works new miracles in this little child. . . .' These are his expressions in nearly every letter. Then comes a more serious preoccupation as he realizes his responsibility and, also, a possible source of fortune in him.

Soon they start their tours, and we have letters from London describing little Wolfgang playing to the King and Queen, and his intention to write an opera for Salzburg to be played by all his little friends. Leopold complains that he is having to incessantly reckon up for him all the young people whom he could enlist for his orchestra. Intrigues and jealousies have already begun. The professional musicians resent the large audiences that Wolfgang attracts, and they are plotting against him. It is not fair.

Before long we come to Wolfgang's own letters. This is on their first Italian journey, and one of the earliest of them is a delightful specimen of childish epistle. ' My very dearest Mama,' it runs, ' my heart is quite enraptured for pure joy, because I feel so merry on this journey, because it is so warm in our carriage, and because our coachman is a brave fellow who drives like the wind wherever the road at all permits it.' A month or two later he ends a letter to his sister, Nannerl, with 'Addio, my children, farewell. I kiss Mama's hand a thousand times, and imprint a hundred little kisses on that wondrous horse-face of thine.' He sends home a charming description of the Carnival in Milan; and from Naples he writes, 'We put on our new clothes yesterday. We were beautiful as angels.'

He shows an acute sense of character already. He writes from Bologna, 'We have the honour of associating with a certain Dominican, who is held to be a holy man. I, indeed, do not altogether believe it, for at breakfast he often takes a cup of chocolate and directly afterwards a good glass of strong Spanish wine; and I have even had the honour of dining with this saint, who drank wine at table with a will and wound up with a whole glass full of strong wine, two good slices of melon, peaches, pears, five bowls of coffee, a whole plate full of cloves, and two full plates of milk with lemons.'

There are many remarks such as, 'To-morrow, my dear sister, we dine out at Herr von Mayer's; and do you know why? Guess! Because he has invited us.' Or, 'Pray, pray, my dear sister, something is biting me—scratch me.'

As he grows older his letters are more informed. They are much longer and more full of serious discussion about his projects and the persons whom he met, but they have, also, just as much of his high spirits as before. He seems to have kept on these same intimate terms of affection with his father and mother and sister. But Leopold's attitude was now more than ever that of task-master. Perhaps he knew that he had neglected one side of his son's character and had never let him have his independence. As a result of this, Wolfgang had no sense of the value of money; and another danger was the quick and easy way in which he fell in love. Also, incredible as it may seem to us, he was lazy. He would never set to work until the last possible moment. And he was not tactful enough. He would not seek out the right people, or pay attention to them.

Of course the truth was that he had been far too long in leading-strings, that he had, very sensibly, been encouraged to do nothing else except his music, and that he had the sort of disposition that could not be happy without affection, and that found its inspiration in the delights and not the sorrows of life. No one, granted the circumstances, could have been a better father to him than Leopold, for his thoughts were entirely and absolutely pre-occupied with his son; and the only criticism that can be brought against Leopold's letters is that he behaved to Wolfgang as if he had never been young himself. He had no understand-ing of Wolfgang's liking for pleasant company during an evening's mild dissipation, and he does not seem to have realized that people who are important socially are not always the most interesting companions. The letters contain many proofs of Wolfgang's knowledge of this truism; as, for instance, when he writes of a certain Count von Salern, at Munich, that 'he understands music, for he always says "bravo" when other cavaliers take a pinch of snuff, sneeze, clear their throats, or begin a conversation.'

Leopold's worries about his son came to a head when Wolfgang made the acquaintance of the Weber family, and fell in love with first one and then the other daughter. His letters are full of admonitions; first of all it was silly to be in love, and then it was the crowning folly of all to wish to get married. He suspected Frau Weber of scheming incessantly to this end; he dreaded her interference in his son's affairs and, in fact, she seems to have played

the traditional rôle of mother-in-law to Leopold
more than she did to Wolfgang, the actual
lover of her daughters.

Wolfgang was at great pains, in his letters,
to explain the successive virtues of first Aloysia
and then Constanze Weber, but Leopold remained unconvinced. In the end, when Wolfgang was forced by Frau Weber to sign a
contract to marry Constanze within three years
or pay her three hundred florins a year, it is
impossible not to sympathize with Leopold in
his disapproval of the whole Weber family.
The inference is that Wolfgang had seduced
Constanze, and though this is none of our
business, there is every reason to believe it was
true. Seduction, in the Weber family, cannot
have been an affair of much difficulty. But it
is, perhaps, lucky that it was Constanze and
not Aloysia whom Wolfgang was to marry. It
must be said to her credit that she quickly tore
up the marriage contract, and that to the best
of her ability she did really love Mozart. Her
character was slight, affectionate, and trivial.
She was obviously no mental companion to her
husband, and even in his first moments of
enthusiasm for her he was unable to claim good
looks for her. All he could say was that ' she
was not ugly, but no one could call her a

beauty, and that her whole advantage consisted in two little black eyes and a graceful figure. Further than that, she had no wit but a little wholesome common sense.' This last quality, it may be added, was just exactly what she did not possess, to any degree whatsoever ; for she had even less sense of money than Wolfgang himself.

They were married without obtaining Leopold's consent. Needless to say, he soon forgave them ; but the marriage broke the close affection of father and son, and they were no longer incessantly in each other's company. On the other hand, this very separation, for the father remained at Salzburg while the son went to live in Vienna, was the reason for a further immense correspondence between them, though, as has been described, all Leopold's share in these letters was destroyed after Mozart's death.

Gradually the situation became one of extreme pathos, for the father grew as hopeless as the son. Indeed, Leopold's last visit to Vienna, in 1785, must have been a time of the most poignant sadness. Leopold knew, by this date, that it was no use, that Wolfgang would never be treated as he deserved. He describes how he listened with tears in his eyes to his son's concerts, and we may well believe it. When he died, not long afterwards, one of the most touching of human relationships had come to an end.

The prevailing note in the remainder of Mozart's letters is of an anguished appeal for loans from rich friends, coupled with an agonized pretence at happiness and optimism so that Constanze, who was by now an apparently permanent invalid, should not be worried. 'You must be pleased to have me back and not worry about money,' were his words, in a letter to Constanze, just after he had written the clarinet concerto, one of his most lovely minor works.

That is typical of his attitude ; but the dark side of the correspondence is in his letters to Michael Puchberg. They abound with such phrases as ' Dearest friend, if you can help with the present pressing expenses, oh, do so ! I have just been obliged to part with my quartet (that difficult work) for a mere song, so as to get ready money. I am now working at some clavier-sonatas for the same reason ' ; or ' Picture my situation—ill and full of care. Could you not assist me with a trifle ? ' Other quotations of the same nature read, ' If you could and would lend me one hundred florins till the twentieth of next month, I should be very much obliged to you. I throw myself on your goodness,' and, 'O God! here am I with fresh entreaties instead of with thanks !— with new demands instead of with payments . . . since you did me that great and friendly service I have lived in such misery that, not only have I not been able to go out, but I could not write for very grief. . . . I am, at the moment, so utterly penniless that I have to beg you, dearest friend, by all that is sacred, to help me with whatever you can spare.'

At the time he was writing these desperate letters he was engaged in a frantic attempt to calm down Constanze and make her think the position less hopeless than it was. His affectionate nature comes out in the strongest colours. 'You would never believe how long the time seems to me since I left you. When I think how merry together we were in Baden, like children. . . . I hope to hold you in my arms on Saturday, perhaps sooner. . . . Tears rained upon the paper as I wrote the foregoing page, but now let us cheer up! Catch! An astonishing number of kisses are flying about. I see a whole crowd of them, too! Ha! Ha! I have just grabbed three—they are delicious!'

An extraordinary personal atmosphere emanates from his letters, and, to close our account of them, we will quote the famous letter to a certain Baron in which he gives precious indications as to his method of work. ' When I am as it were completely myself, entirely alone, and of good cheer—say, travelling in a carriage, or walking after a good meal, or during the night when I cannot sleep ; it is on such occasions that my ideas flow best and most abundantly. Whence and how they come, I know not ; nor can I force them. Those ideas that please me I retain in memory, and am accustomed, as I have been told, to hum them to myself. If I continue in this way, it soon occurs to me how I may turn this or that morsel to account, so as to make a good dish of it, that is to say agreeably to the rules of counterpoint, to the peculiarities of the various instruments, etc.

' All this fires my soul, and, provided I am not disturbed, my subject enlarges itself, becomes methodized and defined, and the whole, though it be long, stands almost complete and finished in my mind, so that I can survey it, like a fine picture or a beautiful statue—at a glance. Nor do I hear in my imagination the parts successively, but I hear them, as it were, all at once. What a delight this is I cannot tell ! All this inventing, this

producing, takes place in a pleasing lively
dream.   Still, the actual hearing of the *tout
ensemble* is, after all, the best.   What has been
thus produced I do not easily forget, and this
is, perhaps, the best gift I have my Divine
Maker to thank for.

'When I proceed to write down my ideas,
I take out of my bag of memory, if I may use
that phrase, what has been previously col-
lected into it in the way I have mentioned.
For this reason the committing to paper is done
quickly enough, for everything is, as I said
before, already finished ; and it rarely differs
on paper from what it was in my imagination.
At this occupation I can, therefore, suffer
myself to be disturbed ; for whatever may be
going on around me, I write, and even talk,
but only of fowls and geese, or of Gretel or
Bärbel, or some such matters.   But why my
productions take from my hand that particular
form and style that makes them Mozartish, and
different from the works of other composers,
is probably owing to the same cause which
renders my nose so large or so aquiline, or, in
short, makes it Mozart's, and different from
those of other people.   For I really do not
study or aim at any originality.'

It will be conceded that this is a unique

account, in his own words, of a great artist at work, and it answers precisely those questions that are most puzzling, such as, for instance, how he managed to compose while people were playing games, or talking on every side of him. This is, necessarily, one of the most interesting of all his letters, but the whole correspondence, for too long kept back from complete translation into our language by an excessive critical prudery, has a real literary value of its own, apart from the fact that it was Mozart who wrote the letters. In fact, he comes out of this correspondence as one of the great letter-writers of the world.

After these evidences, by quotation, of how the truth about his character can be discerned in the words that he wrote, there is just space left to complete the picture of him that we left unfinished at an earlier page of this book. The good looks of his childhood left him in early youth ; his eyes lacked the lustre of genius and were dim, save when he played ; and his nose, as he himself suggests in the letter just quoted, became more aquiline as he grew older, through the greater emaciation and thinness of his face. He died through the excessive strain he imposed upon his nerves and upon his creative power. An improvement in fortune had practically reached him at the moment of his death. It is almost certain that he would have visited, and perhaps lived for some years, in England ; but the temptation to prolong his life in the imagination until, say, the year of Beethoven's death, 1827, when Mozart would have only reached his seventy-first year, is dismissed summarily every time we look at his portrait.

It is not the physique of a long-lived man. Such a man would be delicate now ; and, in his day, people died at so much younger an age. Perhaps he might have lived as long as Chopin, until he was forty, that is to say, and have died some time just before 1800. His life would have been short enough had he lived till then, but the marvels of this final period of his life might well have surpassed all the rest of his achievement.

XI

POSTERITY OF MOZART

' Play Mozart in memory of me—and I will hear you.'

THESE were the last words of Chopin, and
perhaps a hypothetical argument of mutual
admiration might be advanced from this, for
if Chopin loved Mozart, there is, equally, no
doubt whatever that Mozart would have preferred the music of Chopin to that of any other
composer of the succeeding generation. Chopin
will have admired the ease and polish, the
graces and the aristocratic refinements of the
clavier sonatas; but it would be absurd to
look for any traces of their influence in Chopin.
Within their limited scope their form was too
perfected; the Mozart sonata was incapable
of further improvement, and so its fate was to
degenerate in inferior hands. The composer
Hummel was a typical instance of this. He
had been taken to live in Mozart's household,
as a pupil, at the tender age of seven. He
never wrote any work of originality, but he was

a beautiful player, and preserved, it may be supposed, Mozart's style of playing, if nothing more than that.

If we turn from this to chamber-music we find Beethoven imitating Mozart in his early quartets and very quickly emerging from that into his own true stature. That Mozart may have been his model, and the object of his unqualified admiration, did not prevent Beethoven from taking this musical form and making it strictly his own. The six Haydn quartets of Mozart remain, therefore, as a supreme achievement of musical thought, and the Rasumoffsky group, or Beethoven's posthumous quartets, in no sense contradict their eminence, if they equal, or surpass it, in other ways.

But there is a still greater divergence in the symphonies of these two composers, because Beethoven, after a first and a second Mozartian essay, brought a strain of personal suffering and a background of optimistic and unconvincing philosophy into music. His consummate skill has left these embedded there, but they were alien to Mozart. Not a trace of reading is ever to be found in Mozart's music. He was no more learned in that than in the niceties of connoisseurship. Almost the only reference he makes in his letters to anything of the kind is when he writes from Nancy, ' I should like to live here, for the town is indeed charmante—fine houses, fine broad streets, and superb squares.' Except for that, there is but little evidence that he read, or that he ever used his eyes to educate his mind. Except for his Masonic leanings he was completely uninterested in philosophy. He had, therefore, no extraneous optimism, and since only thoughts of a musical texture played through his mind, there is a purity in his music to which Beethoven seldom attained. And it was won with no effort : he had but few pains to arrive at it.

If we turn now to Schubert and try to compare him melodically with Mozart, we come at once into a world of most interesting differences. Schubert, as Liszt so truly said, is the most poetical of all composers that have ever lived. The atmosphere became tainted with poetry whenever the genius of Schubert moved him to write music. It was almost as if poetry were a sweet of some kind, some confection of sugar or Turkish delight that Schubert held in his mouth all the time his inspiration worked. It drugged him. In his moments of divinity, and there were so many of them, Schubert wrote as though his eyes were shut.

The eyes of Mozart were always open ; and

157

he had thought out, beforehand, what he was going to do ; or planned it, at least, into that half-stage whence his extraordinary extempore powers could carry it to completion. But the genius of Schubert burst forth from him in such different manner. The slightest kind of poetry, verse with a good sentiment and the worst execution, rained through him, became transfigured in his imagination into all the beauties of which poetry was capable, and was immediately transformed into music. In Schubert's best chamber-works, in the great trio, in the Trout quintet, and, above all, in the quintet in C, we must recognize qualities that are never to be found in Mozart, and that his good-breeding, we might say, restrained him from feeling.

More particularly the adagio from the quintet in C may be taken as typical of Schubert at the highest moments of his genius, when he was never approached, even by Mozart. It is impossible to listen to this unmoved, there is nothing in the world so poignant ; but, with Mozart, when we get moments of a like intensity, in the heavenly melodies in Figaro, in 'Voi che sapete,' in the letter-duet, in the serenades from Don Giovanni or Il Seraglio, it is different ; it does not climb out of the soil, the poetic action is under a marble portico, or in a moonlit garden. These are two kinds of poetry, with which no written poetry in the world can compare, but one is tied to the fine things of life, and the other does not mind about that and has its eyes shut.

It is the most tragical point in human history that these two men should have died as they did when every mediocrity in their profession was allowed to flourish comfortably. Ditters von Dittersdorf was given a title of nobility and a government post, while Dr. Burney found such an insignificance as the composer Vanhall, 'though somewhat crazed in intellect, living at Vienna in comfortable retirement.' So it is better not to think of the fate of Mozart and of Schubert.

To put it briefly, we find, in Schubert, some one of such prodigious gifts and so meteoric in his output, if not in the actual events of his life, that he falls, naturally, into closer comparison with Mozart than with Beethoven, whose masterpieces were attained with so much more trouble. Mozart and Schubert are the two most convincing instances of genius in the whole of musical history, but Schubert had so pronounced an idiom of his own that it would be vain to seek in it for the evidences of Mozart's direct influence.

The sphere in which this may be found is in opera, and then only in comic opera, or opera buffa. This is because Mozart initiated a new school of comic opera, but only provided it with two models, Figaro and Cosi fan Tutte. There was room, then, for an immense progress upon those lines, but this was only, in the first place, in Italian opera, for, in these two instances, Mozart had constructed masterpieces of the Italian melodic sort, keeping strictly to the principles of Italian comic opera, but improving its scope and enlarging its possible beauties.

It would be natural to start at once with a comparison of the Barber of Seville with Figaro, but Rossini had preluded in this manner, even before that, and L'Italiana in Algeri may be contrasted with Il Seraglio, almost to the advantage of the former. It is certainly more fresh and full of invention, but then Rossini's whole genius was for opera, while opera, and comic opera at that, was only a single facet of Mozart's achievement. There is not a wearying moment in L'Italiana, and there are several, relieved it is true by the most exquisite beauties, in Il Seraglio. It is a pity, indeed, that L'Italiana is never given in England; and its pendant, Il Turco in Italia, which the writer has never heard, is probably just as delightful.

When we come to the Barber of Seville we are in a world of prodigies, once more, for Rossini was only twenty-three years of age and wrote it in the space of a fortnight. The difference between the Barber and Figaro is a difference in breeding, for Rossini wrote as a man in the street; it is less exquisite than Figaro, it is broader and more within ordinary experience. There are no moments of such exquisite character as ' Voi che sapete,' as the Countess's cavatina, or as the letter-duet, but, on the other hand, the characterization by music is just as complete, and the opening chorus, ' piano, pianissimo,' the serenade, the music-lesson, are inventions on a high plane of poetry.

The atmosphere is fixed, is secured, by the use of recitative, and its lovely modulations make an enhancement of the scene, so that the worst kind of scenery goes unnoticed, even when one of Rossini's lovely airs is not being sung, and there is a lovely song at every moment. Such an unimportant thing as the old housemaid's song in the third Act, which is sometimes omitted in performance, is a moment wonderful in itself and tinged with a sort of solemn poetry as though we were really being taken back to that old, sleepy civilization and were being given our proofs of its realities in the smallest detail. 'Buona sera, mio signore' is a song of creeping, Jesuitical excuse, an invasion by casuistry, marvellously expressed in music.

What more can be said of the Barbiere ! It was written as a dangerous comparison, and it triumphed ; as of who should write a companion-piece to the Magic Flute and not disgrace himself in the process. But it has become more a part of everyday experience ; in Figaro, the Count and Countess Almaviva are like the rulers of a small German State, they are as important in their minor way as the Prince-Archbishop from whom Mozart had suffered at Salzburg. In the Barbiere the characters are poorer persons ; they are rich citizens in a rather decaying town. In Figaro, they are wealthy enough to afford every luxury, and the atmosphere is that of a Court. In the Barbiere, the prosperity is ebbing away and the chief comfort is from the climate, warmly expressed in the flowering of so many pretty tunes.

The ordinary person's experience of Rossini begins and ends with the Barbiere, but the

operatic genius of both Rossini and Mozart
found its greatest development in the same
direction, so that while Mozart carried on the
opera buffa from Figaro to Cosi fan Tutte,
Rossini wrote several comic operas after the
Barbiere, but, unfortunately for the public,
they are never performed. Cenerentola and
Gazza Ladra are familiar only through their
overtures, but they abound in beautiful airs,
comical situations, and scenic possibilities, and
all their virtues are in direct descendance from
Mozart.

Rossini, who was, at the same time, too lazy
and too busy for anything else, had a predi-
lection for Mozart, and, it may be added, for
Haydn. Apart from this, so far as he had
modelled himself upon anything, Rossini had
adapted the methods of Paesiello and Cima-
rosa ; and it was from these two composers
that Mozart had stolen his fire for Figaro and
Cosi fan Tutte. ' Whoever seeks for light and
pleasurable sensations in music cannot be re-
commended to anything better than Paesiello,'
were Mozart's own words ; and light and
pleasurable sensations were the aim of the
Italian opera buffa.

The Barbiere, Cenerentola, Gazza Ladra,
L'Italiana in Algeri, these were familiar to all

Europe a century ago. They were played from every bandstand, and in every café, and there was no drawing-room cultured enough to possess a piano that did not have some of Rossini's airs lying open upon the music-stand, as though incessantly consulted. His genius was compared to that of Leonardo or Titian; now he is most unjustly neglected, while Wagner, whose loud vulgar personality and unpleasant literary associations should have perished long ago, is still played. Yet, of Wagner and Rossini, as of Wagner and Verdi, it is perfectly evident who was an artist and who was nothing of the kind. The old Italian opera was a beautiful thing, before Wagner, and the comic operas of Rossini were its finest ornament after those of Mozart.

Nor were Rossini's essays in comic opera confined to the early part of his experience, while he still lived in Italy. When he moved to Paris, before the production of William Tell and his sensational retirement into private life at only thirty-eight years of age, he wrote a French comic opera, Il Conte Ory. It is probable that this has never been performed anywhere since the reign of Napoleon III., but the best contemporary judges refer to it as Rossini's supreme masterpiece in comic opera.

Liszt, who mounted it at Weimar, was a particular admirer of its beauties. He describes its melodies as 'flowing like champagne.' The situations were of the order of those in Figaro and Cosi fan Tutte ; and a great many of Rossini's most beautiful inventions lie, forgotten for ever it would seem, in this neglected opera.

A comic opera by another composer, in which the influence of Mozart is most evident, is Don Pasquale by Donizetti. This delightful entertainment is still given, fairly frequently, in Italy and in Germany, and its easiness, grace and rapidity must alter any adverse opinion of Donizetti. Light and pleasurable sensations are here so admirably expressed and so easily absorbed that it becomes difficult to take the more serious view of the purposes of opera. The overture to Don Pasquale is a perfect example of what the prelude to a comic opera should be ; it is as neat and rapid as that to Cosi fan Tutte, and it distils just as convincing an atmosphere of what is to follow. The personages are as difficult to part from as those in Figaro, and one is left hoping to meet them again one day.

The last flickerings of the tradition are to be found in Offenbach. There are moments

in La Vie Parisienne where no one who loves
Mozart could fail to see his shadow.   More
particularly is this so in the letter-song, where
Metella reads aloud the letter sent her by the
Baron de Gondremark, which has been cast
by Offenbach into the most exquisite rondo.
The whole of La Vie Parisienne has life of a
most peculiar kind ; it is such a study of a
moment in time that it has been left suspended ;

> ' Je veux, moi, dans la capitale,
> Voir les divas qui font fureur,
> Voir la Patti dans Don Pasquale
> Et Thérèsa dans Le Sapeur ' ;

so runs the song of the beautiful Baroness de
Gondremark in the first Act.   Those words are
typical of the whole piece ; the exact moment
of 1867 is put before us by the genius of Offenbach.   The third scene, when the fête takes
place, rises to a level near to that of the banquet
scene in Don Giovanni.   The ghost-like comic
characters, ghost-like because they are so im-
probable, and Gardefeu and Bobinet, and all
the supernumeraries put there by Meilhac and
Halévy, the librettists, all these are participants
in the orgy.   No one but Offenbach could
write music like this ; the slangy waltzes are
like the clatter and clang of orchestras escaping

when the swing-doors of the theatre are opened
for a moment, and there are polkas, galops,
redowas, succeeding one another as do the tunes
at Don Juan's banquet. Then the Baron de
Gondremark is crowned with a wreath of rose-
leaves, and this is always, in Offenbach, the
occasion for a frenzied renewal of all the whirl-
ing rhythms, a quadrille made out of all the
tunes of the piece. The Bacchanale at the end of
Orphée aux Enfers is a moment of the same kind.

La Vie Parisienne is the summarized life of
its time in the way that Figaro or Cosi fan
Tutte are the expression of their own epoch.
We find Mozart's clichés, the serenades, the
letter-songs, the cavatinas, the ensembles, all
over again, but with a magnified force, for
Offenbach demands a large orchestra, and he
was an admirer of Berlioz. If we knew La
Périchole as well as we know La Vie Parisienne,
with its fête-music for the Viceroy, its entracte-
valses, its boleros, serenades, and galop finales,
we should feel again how much this man, who
seems to have slept and eaten in the theatre,
owed to Mozart. Vert-Vert, or another opera,
Le Roi Carotte, waltz after waltz, rondo,
redowa, serenade, are other examples of Offenbach at his best ; or Madame l'Archiduc, or
Madame Favart with its Tyroliennes and

167

waltzes, or La Fille du Tambour-Major with its military marches and its tarantella, these all belong to a dead and forgotten world. It had so much more vitality than any American music has ever possessed, and it was founded on the models of Mozart and Rossini. Not only is it dead, but it can never be properly revived, for the particular art of singing it has died.

And then we arrive at Johann Strauss, who perfected the Viennese accent, and in Fledermaus reached to the speed and the flowing, sinuous line of the ensembles in Figaro. It is impossible to think of any piece of music that Mozart, himself, would have enjoyed more than the overture to this ; it is so much more in his spirit than Beethoven. The form of the whole opera came directly through the books set by Offenbach, and was derived in direct descent from Da Ponte. But, for all this, Strauss had not the variety and the scope of Offenbach ; his forte was the Viennese waltz, and he had, perhaps, more delicacy and more feeling, but less force and less invention than Offenbach. And Fledermaus was by far his best achievement ; his other pieces fall far short of it and are to be distinguished only by an exceptional waltz, as, for instance, in the Night in Venice, or in Wiener Blut.

So, if the posterity of Mozart was fruitless, eventually, in every other branch of music, it produced this great school of comic opera, and we are left with the conviction that had Mozart lived to anything approaching a normal span of life, his career would have been in opera. This was always his ambition. It failed, as did every other prospect that he embarked upon ; but, where he had said, in his short life, as much as he had to say upon every other subject, opera was a sphere into which he had hardly advanced. It had many branches, but two main divisions, German and Italian opera, between which he was always, himself, hesitating. The echoes of his two experiments in comic opera continued for some two generations after his death, until Wagner appeared. With the arrival of that new force an interesting phase of life was pushed out of existence, and this fact is coming slowly into recognition and brings with it a feeling of resentment against Wagner, and a wish to hear more of Rossini, of Offenbach, and of Verdi. In the end, their beauties must survive his blatant vulgarities and his tweed-clad tunes.

XII

SOME LITTLE-KNOWN MASTERPIECES

In this final chapter it is proposed to give a few details about some of Mozart's more rarely heard works. Among these, the most beautiful of his instrumental compositions are to be found, but they are in a rare category by themselves, and the enthusiasts who wish to hear them have to keep a careful watch on concert programmes, and, even then, are too often disappointed, for some of these pieces, though they are Mozart at his best, are practically never performed.

We will begin with the serenades, or divertimenti. Two of these have a universal fame—the Haffner Serenade in D (K. 250), and Eine Kleine Nachtmusik (K. 525). Everyone knows them, so there is little point in discussing their beauties, beyond observing that the last dates from 1787, the very best period of Mozart. It will be more profitable to mention the Nocturne in F written for a fête given by Countess Lodron, who will be remembered as the lady with two daughters for whom Mozart wrote the concerto for three pianofortes. The Nocturne is in six movements, and forms one of the best specimens of his Rococo style. There is, also, the second divertimento, a septuor written for his sister's birthday, in five movements, à la française, in French style, that is to say, with a spirited march at the beginning and end. The Haffner Serenade was written at the same time as this ; it was the year 1776.

Another piece from about the same period is a divertimento for string-quartet and two horns. It has a beautiful andante, two minuets in French style, of which the first became a popular dance-tune at Paris, and a finale with effects of hunting-horns in the manner of Gossec and Grétry. In the following year he wrote a Nocturne (K. 286) for four orchestras, each consisting of two violins, one viola, bass, and two horns, by means of which a triple echo was produced. The effect of this must be curious, if not beautiful. Two lovely serenades for wind-instruments date from his first arrival in Vienna, after he had left Salzburg, in 1781. There is, also, a most lively and charming serenade for thirteen wind-instruments ; and the musical joke for string-quartet and two

horns (K. 522) must be indicated. This dates
from 1787, and parodies a village-band.

We will turn aside, now, to another branch
of his activity—his instrumental trios. Five of
these date from his best period of production.
Two of them, (K. 496) and (K. 564), were
adapted quickly, in view of some forthcoming
party, from pianoforte solos, but, in spite of
this, it would be difficult to imagine anything
more lovely in its effect than the latter of these,
with the Sicilienne of heavenly beauty, with
which it ends. That in E major (K. 542),
perhaps the finest of the series, was written for
a party given by the merchant Puchberg, who
was continually making loans to Mozart. In
June 1788, he writes to Puchberg, ' When can
we have a little music at your house ? I have
written a new Trio.' The clarinet trio (K.
498) is a beautiful thing, too ; and, altogether,
in these trios, the simplicity of the form inspired Mozart to some of his most limpid and
flowing poetry. No music could be more
admirably adapted to its purpose, and it is a
miraculous gift to have Mozart in the very room,
as it were, while these lovely trifles are performed
over which no one, save Mozart, would have spent
so much care or given so freely of his talent.

A whole series of compositions for the flute

must be considered together, because they all date from his residence in Paris, in 1778. These works comprise three flute quartets, two flute concertos, and an andante for flute and orchestra. Mozart disliked the flute very much indeed, but it was much in favour with the French amateurs ; and so he made use of it, and his works for the flute are necessarily French in colouring and atmosphere. But the best of the series is the concerto for flute and harp (K. 299), which was written for the Duc de Guines and his daughter, to whom Mozart gave music-lessons. There are some amusing letters about this father and daughter, and she seems to have been an excellent performer. Mozart did not like the harp any more than he cared for the flute ; though there are no traces of it in the concerto, which is a charming con-versation-piece, in the sense that it renders so well an elegant assembly of people and the delicacies with which their ears are flattered while they can be constrained to stop talking, just for a few moments. This concerto is still given, and is, perhaps, more effective in its associations than in actual content, for these two instruments, in spite of their lovely sound and the mastery with which they are employed, make an unsatisfactory combination.

Another instance in which he employed a part of his resources over a single instrument is the horn, for which he wrote four concertos and a quintet, chiefly in the years 1782 and 1783. They were written for Joseph Leutgeb, a native of Salzburg, who was a good player, but a kind of buffoon of Mozart's. The last of the concertos (K. 495), composed in 1786, was written down in red, blue, black, and green inks, and the margin of the manuscript is full of jokes at Leutgeb's expense. But the effect of, at any rate the second of these works (K. 417), the only one of them known to the writer, is most beautiful. The rondo with which it ends has flourishes as of hunting-horns, and is a delightful little instance of Mozart's imagination and poetic sense. I have never heard the horn quintet (K. 407), but this is, in all probability, a more serious work, and it should take rank with the oboe quartet and the quintet for piano and wind. It is in the customary quartet style, and may be extremely beautiful.

There is, also, a bassoon concerto (K. 191), dating from 1774, the only survivor of a series of three, for the other two are lost ; it is never impossible, though, that they may, one day, be recovered. This must be the first serious use made of the bassoon as a solo-instrument, and this concerto for it, which was written while he composed his lovely violin concertos, is an example of how Mozart could give his most serious consideration, and the benefits of his loveliest inspirations, to whatever small work was under his hand at the moment.

Attention has just been drawn, a few lines back, to the oboe quartet and the quintet for piano and wind, but, in fact, the oboe plays the leading part in both these compositions. The first of them (K. 370) dates from 1781, and the second, in E flat (K. 452), from 1784. Both are masterpieces, and they could not conceivably be improved upon. They were written with particular players in view, and they show off the character of the instruments to perfection and invest them with all the poetry of which their uses are capable. The oboe quartet is of magical beauty, and the psychology of the instrument has been studied with extraordinary care and instinct. The wind-quintet is, perhaps, even finer. It is scored for the delightful combination of piano, oboe, clarinet, horn, and bassoon ; and wind-instruments have never been treated with such delicacy and fancy, even by Schubert in his Octet. The slow movement of this wind-quintet is the exceptional thing of the whole work. It is of truly ravishing loveliness.

Mozart, himself, was particularly pleased with the whole work and describes it to his father as the best thing he had yet written.

Most certainly, both this and the oboe quartet are among the most delightful things ever done by Mozart. They have, of necessity, less intellectual content than the quartets and quintets that he wrote for the ordinary, orthodox combinations of instruments, and are the expression, therefore, of a particular occasion more than an opportunity for severe musical thinking. Their spirit, in fact, is that of his trios ; they were written for special players at an evening party in the house of some friend or patron of Mozart. They were meant to delight the ear, and they carry in their melodious strains a suggestion of the cooling and delicate refreshments at the end of the concert—the ices, the fruits, the light wines, and the tokay.

In comparison with them, there is a greater seriousness in the works that Mozart wrote for the clarinet. These are two in number, a quintet and a concerto, and they were composed, without any hope of profit, for Anton Stadler, a good musician, but a man of disreputable character who lived upon Mozart, borrowed money from him, made Mozart pawn his valuables when no other money was available, and, in all probability, led him into bad habits as his drinking companion. The quintet (K. 581) was written in September 1789, at a very low ebb in Mozart's fortunes, when Constanze's long illness had begun, and when his own debts were mounting dangerously high. Yet it is difficult to think of any more superb example of Mozart than the first movement of this quintet. It is Italian in style ; in the way that Figaro or Cosi fan Tutte are Italian, and in the sense that Wagner described Mozart's symphonies as being Italian. It is not, that is to say, so much authentically Italian in texture, but it partakes of an idealized Italian character, and it possesses those qualities that could be looked for in Italy and never found. The clarinet quintet of Brahms, almost comparable to it in loveliness, forms a contrast of the most absorbing interest. It is almost the last work of Brahms, and was written when he was nearly sixty years of age, and in the full use of his talents. Brahms has made use of the mysterious qualities of the instrument ; its tones are hidden, they are remote and veiled ; they sound through the trees, or across water ; there is even a hint of the Orient in his treatment of the instrument ; its direct contingencies are not expressed as they are by Mozart. So lovely is this first movement of the Mozart quintet that the succeeding movements rather lose in comparison with it ; and it is this inequality in its pieces that, in the end, makes the Brahms as fine a work as the Mozart, though never, through all its length, is it as beautiful as Mozart in his beginning.

The clarinet concerto (K. 622) was composed by Mozart, in 1791, not more than a month or two before his death. Indeed, it is his latest instrumental work. He wrote it specially for Stadler, who was going to seek his fortune in Prague, and, in addition to this concerto, Mozart provided him with money for his expenses and with letters of recommendation. Although written so near to his death-bed, the concerto shows no signs of weakness. It has lovely themes, it shows Mozart's extraordinary attention to detail and his innate understanding of the qualities of any instrument he treated, and it is the classical work for the clarinet, having never been superseded.

Even after the enumeration of all these different pieces there still remain many things that cannot be ignored and that demand mention. There are Mozart's songs, rising from the simplest little lieder, some of them written at the end of his life, as, for instance, the three little songs that he wrote for a children's paper in 1791, to great and formal arias constructed not so much like a song as a concerto for voice and orchestra. Probably the greatest of these are 'Io non chiedo' (K. 316), written for Aloysia Weber when he was in love with her, and abounding in great coloratura effects, and 'Bella mia fiamma' (K. 528), composed in 1787, while he was in Prague for the production of Don Giovanni.

Another division of his works is concerned with his Masonic interests. In 1783 he wrote a Masonic cantata (K. 429), another one (K. 471) two years later, and, on his very death-bed, a little cantata (K. 623) for a new lodge of Masons. Three weeks before he died he had just strength enough to drag himself from bed and conduct its first performance. Whatever may be the character of these works, there can be no doubt as to the importance of the Masonic Funeral March (K. 477). This was composed, in 1785, for the funeral of a member of the Esterhazy family. It is music of a grave, mysterious import, and is far from being the least of Mozart's works.

Finally, at the very end of his career, there comes the little group of works for the mechani-

cal-organ and for the glass-harmonica. Two
of these are among the noblest works of Mozart.
They are said to be essays in the styles of Handel
and of Bach, but they may be more truly
described as explorations into a new direction.
No one who has ever heard the Fantasia in F
minor (K. 608) could describe it as an experiment by Mozart in the style of some other
composer. On the contrary, it is one of his
last and more serious experiments ; and the
wonder remains how Mozart could have raised
these pieces of so trivial a destination to so
high a level of thought and utterance.

It is highly probable that the quintet for
glass-harmonica (K. 617), with oboe, flute,
viola, and violoncello, may be among the most
lovely of all Mozart's smaller works. It may
be the equal of the oboe quartet, the quintet
for piano and wind, and the horn quintet ; and
in case this should be so, it is important that it
should be, somehow, revived, in the way, for
instance, that Schubert's sonata for another
lost instrument, the arpeggione, has been
rescued by M. Gaspar Cassado, the 'cellist.
It will be remembered, too, that Gluck played
a concerto of his own composition for musical-
glasses during his visit to England in 1746 ;
and the importance and value of all Mozart's

experiments in unusual musical forms demand
that this quintet, one of the last of his long list
of compositions, should be adapted to performance. Neither Mozart nor Gluck des-
pised this quaint kind of instrument, and that
should be sufficient excuse for its revival.

There is now, perhaps, hardly anything of
importance by Mozart that has not been, at
least, mentioned, and we are given a late
opportunity to consider our verdict upon him.
How are we to compare him with Bach, or
with Beethoven? In his third and ninth
symphonies, in sonata op. III, in the three Rasumoffsky quartets, and in the five posthumous
quartets, Beethoven reaches beyond Mozart,
but it was only after years of heroical energy.
His genius was not adaptable as that of Mozart.
He had not Mozart's interest in the timbre and
in the particular properties of different instruments. He had more force than Mozart, but
he was lacking in poetry and in sense of beauty,
so that his greatest achievements were in the
mechanical, the mathematical perfection of his
shapes. In his highest moments, the deity was
the machine itself, and not the divinity im-
prisoned in it. With Mozart there was always
poetry inside the engine, but with Beethoven
it was the engine itself: and the nicety of its

working produced an optimism which the success of his heroic attempts, and the penalty of his terrible labours, made to appear in the guise of a sentimental philosophy, without any guarantees, and based on the assumption that because he suffered he must be right. There can be no question of Mozart's greater subtlety of thought and higher natural equipment. This is implicit in even the smallest things that he did. His range was greater ; his sense of beauty greater ; he understood human character (and Beethoven never did); in his supreme moments he floated easily where Beethoven climbed to with difficulty ; he had elegance which Beethoven never possessed ; and he pronounced with certainty, truths that Beethoven took, blindly, on assurance.

But Mozart has not quite this supremacy when he is compared with Bach. The wonders of Mozart's youth, the fact that he could compose music almost before he could speak, are paralleled by the astonishing musical descent of Bach and his inherited facility. The question of their respective dates is important. Wren must always be a greater architect than Robert Adam, Rubens be a greater painter than Fragonard ; for the Baroque is, ever, on a greater scale than the Rococo. But it is no use to compare Bach with any other artist from the North, in any of the arts. The regularity of his mental processes is the most astounding achievement of the human race, for the forms seem to have taken instant shape from him, every day. He stood between the past and the future and was the summary of them both, so that he belongs equally to his own century, to the sixteenth century, and to the century that is yet to come. This can not be said of Mozart, who was an end in himself, and had no posterity. There is this other difference between them, that we can never think of Bach as young, or Mozart as old ; yet if we expect nothing from Mozart but youthfulness and exquisite grace we are profoundly mistaken, for he had the mastery of all forms. I do not think, though, that his physique would have let him live to be old ; even had his fate been more fortunate, perhaps he would have died soon after his fortieth year.

The fibre of Bach's thought was stronger than that of Mozart, and his giant strength was alien to this younger, slighter man, whose music, if it started as quickly as that of Bach, was more quickly stopped. For there is an end to all things, and however much we love Mozart we must not make this heaven of refuge into our permanent dwelling-place. We must look into the future, as well as into the niceties of that perfected past, and after much Mozart we may want Berlioz. He had qualities which no other musician has ever had—except Bach ; and so, if we return to Bach, it is to acknowledge that Mozart was second to him. There we can leave him.

BIBLIOGRAPHICAL NOTE

In writing this life of Mozart it is sufficient to say that all the authorities available to me have been consulted. His earliest biographer, Edward Holmes, has proved as invaluable as he is excellent, but it is necessary, also, to mention with particular warmth the lives of Mozart by Dyneley Hussey and by Henri de Curzon. The former, more especially, it would be difficult to improve upon for its manner and treatment, while in the latter the marshalling of facts is from the hand of a real master of statistics. On many aspects of Mozart Professor Dent is the final authority, and it is, therefore, superfluous to acknowledge an unavoidable debt to his wisdom and understanding. Saint-Foix and de Wyzewa have also been consulted, but perhaps their division of Mozart's first twenty years of existence into no fewer than thirty-three separate phases of influence and production is a little serious-minded. Of the numerous other authorities it is unnecessary to say much, except that no one who attempts to write a life of Mozart can omit to consult the notices upon him in the *Encyclopaedia Britannica*, in Grove's *Musical Dictionary*, and in Cobbett's *Cyclopaedic Survey of Chamber-Music*.

So much of Mozart's early life consists of anecdote that the author must apologize to his public for the inclusion of many stories as familiar as that of King

Alfred and the cakes. Fresh information about Mozart it is impossible to acquire, but it is hoped that in these pages something new may have been attempted in two other directions. It is claimed by the author that he has devoted more attention than any previous writer upon the subject to the civilization in which Mozart lived, being the author of the only book in our language that deals with the art and architecture of Austria and Germany at that time. This has been, therefore, an unrivalled opportunity to analyse the parallels to Mozart's music in the other arts of the day. Further, he has tried to convey the atmosphere of his music, to examine what things may have been in his brain when he wrote it, and to state what effect it produces upon sensitive, if untrained, ears. Otto Jahn, in his monumental work upon Mozart, if he has omitted nothing else, has not attempted this. To that small extent, then, there may be something new in these pages. Finally, the author wishes to repair an omission inadvertently made in the earlier copies of this book, and to place on record his indebtedness to the edition of *The Letters of Mozart*, edited by Hans Mersmann and admirably translated by M. M. Bozman, and published by Messrs. J. M. Dent & Sons Ltd. This is the only English translation of Mozart's letters, and is, of course, invaluable to any student of the subject.

Note.—*The letter* K, *followed by a number, refers to the* Köchel *index of Mozart's works.*

INDEX

INDEX